First published in Great Britain in 2010 by
HEADLINE PUBLISHING GROUP

3

Cataloguing in Publication Data is available from the British Library

ISBN 978 0 7553 6070 3

Typeset in Rotis Sans Serif by Avon DataSet Ltd,
Bidford-on-Avon, Warwickshire

Printed and bound in Great Britain by
Clays Ltd, St Ives plc

Headline's policy is to use papers that are natural, renewable and
recyclable products and made from wood grown in sustainable forests.
The logging and manufacturing processes are expected to conform
to the environmental regulations of the country of origin.

HEADLINE PUBLISHING GROUP
An Hachette UK Company
338 Euston Road
London NW1 3BH

www.headline.co.uk
www.hachette.co.uk

WHAT'S YOUR BRIGHT IDEA?
THE JOURNEY TO STARTING YOUR OWN BUSINESS

Tim Campbell and Paul Humphries

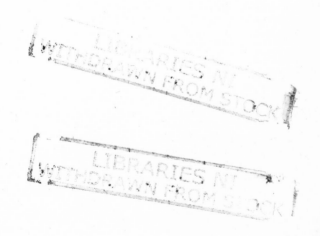

headline
business plus

CONTENTS

PREFACE

Making a Change

A few years ago, the opportunity was given to the younger of the two authors of this book, Tim Campbell, to get into business when he won the first BBC *The Apprentice* series.

When he applied to go on the show he was a project manager working at Transport for London. A few weeks later, having won the contest, Tim was propelled into the privileged position of working alongside the then Sir Alan Sugar at Amstrad where he learned a great deal about what it takes to get going in business.

During this time he realised that while more and more people are looking to start their own business, it's still not always that easy, even for those who are passionate about it and particularly for those who are trying to start their own business for the first time. Access to information, experience, knowledge and finance can still be more difficult than it should be in the UK.

A Real Apprenticeship

When Tim left Amstrad to start up his own business, it became even more evident to him that there is a real need for support. He wanted to start his own business but how should he turn his bright idea into a workable business plan? Where could he find trusted advice and guidance he knew he needed? How would he raise the funding required to get things off the ground? And what did he need to do, and in which order, to get going?

Tim and Paul first met around this time. We quickly found that the blend of Tim's youthful enthusiasm, drive and ambition to succeed in business blended well with Paul's years of experience of running start-up and early-stage businesses. Together we worked on the development of a number of new business ideas, rejecting some along the way and eventually successfully launching a couple – more of those later. We also established a charitable social enterprise called Bright Ideas Trust, an organisation that helps young people to start their own businesses by supporting them with a financial investment, entrepreneurial mentoring and business education programmes.

Tim calls this his 'real' apprenticeship: the first opportunity to start to understand for the first time how the business of running your own business works, what all the jargon means, that it's not that complicated when you start to learn what you're doing. Importantly, he saw for the first time that being an entrepreneur is not just for a select few talented individuals. As one business guru put it: 'Entrepreneurship isn't about being crazy and creative and a big risk-taker. Nowadays, it's been proven that entrepreneurship can be taught as a systematic, replicable process'.[1] It's a mindset and an attitude with a focus on getting things done and one that almost anyone can have. So this book aims to pass on some of the knowledge and experience gained in this apprenticeship.

Our Journey

If Tim had a pound for every person who approached him asking for advice and guidance during this period he'd be worth almost as much as Lord Sugar himself.

As mentioned, the idea behind this book came out of the journey that Tim took when he first left Amstrad and wanted to set up his own business. It's also based on the journey Paul took when he left his big company career after fifteen years to embark upon setting up his own business. We had different starting points, different

---

1   Jim Collins

destinations in mind, were at different stages of life but embarked on essentially the same journey.

Actually, we're both still very much on that journey and are continuing to learn about the world of business every day. In both cases we looked around for some practical guidance from people who had been down this road before. And while we found a lot of stuff out there, we never really felt that we were getting right to the heart of what's important when starting your own business. So this book is based on very recent and real experience of doing this having known little about what's involved in starting a business venture when we started out. It's fresh in the mind. It tries to focus on the big and important things rather than go into the minute details and the less critical aspects of starting your own business – so you just get the most of what you really need.

GETTING THE URGE
– WANDERLUST!

THE JOURNEY

Wanderlust: 'a strong desire for or impulse to wander, or, in modern usage, to travel and to explore the world'

> If you're reading this book the chances are that you are seriously thinking about starting up and running your own business. Or maybe you've already started and are looking for some inspiration or just advice and guidance to help you along. Or maybe you're just curious to see if it might be the right road for you.

Why Read This?

Whatever stage you're at we want to help you to make the best use of your time, energy, resources, creativity and passion by giving you an insight into what our experiences have taught us about starting up a business. Think of starting your own business as being like setting out on a journey or a great adventure. For many, it has become not just a journey of a lifetime but a life-changing experience. Once they've taken this path, business owners often say that they never want to do anything else and that they could not imagine going to work for someone else in the future.

At this stage the thought may also have crossed your mind that starting your own business might range from being complicated through to near impossible. There's a whole industry out there that would like to make it seem more difficult than it really is. While business does have many complexities, at the heart of it are a few key things that, done well, will lead to success. And like so many things, when you know what you're doing, it's relatively straightforward. Like riding a bike or driving a car – think back to when you couldn't do these things. You'll make mistakes, get frustrated, maybe fall off or, even worse, crash, but what you will do to help you get there is to focus on the basic principles detailed in the chapters ahead.

Our Aim

In the last few years we've been approached by hundreds of would-be first-time business owners looking for advice and support on how to get started.

This book is aimed at helping to inspire you to start on the great journey that is setting up, owning and running your own business. It's a journey to be relished and enjoyed, a real adventure on which you will learn a huge amount about yourself and other people and hopefully provide you with a good livelihood and the income that you want. But it also involves considerable hard work and can be fraught with potholes just waiting to be hit.

So we also aim to provide some signposts to help you to navigate through the first stages of a lifetime's journey – the steps that will take you from having a bright idea to being ready to launch. And to point out some of the pitfalls that you may encounter and give you guidance on how to avoid or overcome these.

We're often asked whether or not anyone can set up and run their own business. Are entrepreneurs born or made? Do I need a unique and brilliant business idea to be successful? How do I know that my idea will work or that I'm on the right lines? Where can I get the help that I need? So this book came about because so many people have approached us over the last few years to ask our advice on how they get started in business. We will answer these questions in the pages that follow.

We believe that many, even most, can do it. But not all. We believe that you do *not* need a brilliant idea, just a reasonably good one that meets a few basic criteria and which is capable of being well delivered by you. We think that entrepreneurs, in the purest sense of the word, are probably born, but that *business owners* can be made – we'll talk about the difference later. We believe that you will have a better chance of success if you do the right things and that creating a business is in large part a set of replicable activities rather than the work of genius with a sprinkle of magic dust. Hence, many can do it, not just 'entrepreneurs'. This book aims to stimulate, inform and inspire a new generation to choose the business ownership path.

Replicable Approach

There are many different ways to realise your business ownership dreams. If you take anything from reading this book, our hope is that it would be this – despite what many would have you believe, there are only a few rules that you need to follow when starting your own business. For the most part you can be successful in any number of different ways, so do not be constrained by thinking that you have to do it the way that someone else did it. Like any journey you can just set off and see where things take you. There is no definitive right or wrong way – just *your* way. So that part is really up to you.

But at the same time there are many things that you can do, and some things to avoid, which will give you a better chance at success, based on the common successes and failings of many new businesses that we've seen or been involved with. There are some straightforward approaches, processes and tools and techniques that you should stick fairly closely to to give you a better chance – these are the replicable bits. So we would argue that setting up your own business is about 80 per cent common to all businesses and perhaps 20 per cent variable depending upon your specific business. So we will focus on the ways to do the 80 per cent that is required. To help with that, this book is organised into five sections. Each section covers a major stage in the process to get you from your first stirrings that business ownership might be right for you through to the time when you are ready to launch. These stages are outlined in the diagram (below) that we'll return to through the following pages.

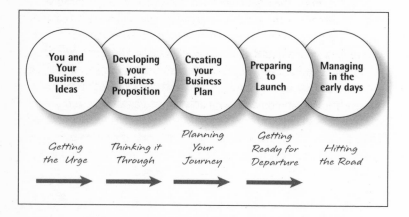

Proper Planning Prevents Poor Performance

It's an old cliché but nonetheless true – businesses usually do work out better if you take time to plan them. If you've got no experience of planning, don't worry – much of this book deals with ways that you can do these things and gives you some practical tips along the way to speed you on your journey. If you are a veteran of planning then we hope that this will provide you with a refresher and maybe even show you some things that you haven't thought of or done before as well as some new approaches.

Most good journeys, and especially journeys of a lifetime, will require some form of planning. The amount of planning may vary depending upon your character, experience and desires. But to get the most out of it, the journey needs a purpose, objectives or goals, a map, an itinerary and some experienced guidance. Most successful business ventures did not achieve that success by accident – they were usually well thought through, carefully planned and rigorously implemented and managed.

We've used the techniques we talk about many times ourselves. We can show you what works for us and let you decide if some of these approaches might be right for you. Sometimes we created a business that went on to be successful, sometimes very successful. Sometimes it led us to decide that while the idea might have looked good at the outset, there was no viable business to launch and we stopped and saved our time and money. Either way, if you want to start a business and get it off on the right track then the following pages will give you the benefit of the wisdom of many people we have worked with who have gone down this road before. And while it's inevitable that everyone will occasionally take a wrong turn and encounter unfortunate events along the way, there are a number of things that you can do to help to get you on the right track to turning your business idea – and dream – into a business reality.

CAN YOU DO IT?

'The first step towards getting somewhere is to decide that you are not going to stay where you are.' Anon

So you think you want to run your own business. Before you go charging off down the road let's take a look at whether you are the right person for this journey. So this section looks at some of the characteristics and personal qualities that can help you to be successful at running your own business, and hopefully to help you to decide if it's right for you. It looks at where you could be starting your journey from and describes how running your own business can satisfy a number of personal motivations for choosing this path.

Is it Up Your Street?

Am I right for owning my own business? And can I do it? These are questions that you will rightly be asking yourself before setting out. You will be pleased to hear that there is a good chance that the answers will be 'Yes'. History clearly shows that people from a very wide range of different experiences and backgrounds have done it successfully. The fact that there are currently nearly five million[2] small businesses in the UK demonstrates that business owners are not all from the same mould – it takes all sorts. But it's also not for everyone, as we will see. So how can you know if it's for you?

The bald answer is that you cannot know until you have a go. You can try filling out self-assessment forms or doing psychometric tests. You can go on training courses. You can ask people who know you if they think that you could do it. That's all good stuff but ultimately you will just need to have self-belief and give it a go. One word of caution though – this is not a journey that should be taken lightly. To say that 'anyone can do it' would be to falsely raise expectations and would be irresponsible of us.

In the course of our work at Bright Ideas Trust, we are often asked by budding young business owners if we think that they will be capable of running their own business. They may have a good idea and bags of motivation and energy but some of them are looking for reassurance on this. We can't tell them what the outcome of their efforts might be, but we can tell you some of the personal qualities that you will require to be successful.

Personal Qualities

Each of us has a set of characteristics that make us who we are – our inherent personal qualities along with the skills and experience developed and gained in life and work so far. There is no perfect set of characteristics to be successful in business. So ask yourself, 'Do I have what it takes?' This question will include some or all of the following personal qualities that are required day-to-day to run your own business:

2   FSB Small Business Guide 2010

■ *DISCIPLINE AND ROUTINE* – Can I make a plan and then follow it through? Can I focus on achieving my goals even when there are other things to do that look interesting or appealing that might distract from my aim?

■ *DILIGENCE* – Do I like to apply myself to tasks and see them through to the end result, even if the going gets tough and it's easier to give up and move on to something else?

■ *TRUSTWORTHINESS AND HONESTY* – Do I care about delivering to other people what I promise them and am reliable with my own and other people's money?

■ *PUNCTUALITY AND RELIABILITY* – Do I appreciate the importance of committing to other people that I will do things at a set time and then consistently meet this commitment? Do I dislike being late and do all I can to avoid this?

■ *ORGANISATION AND EFFICIENCY* – Do I like to get things organised? Do I routinely look for ways and get pleasure out of finding ways to do things better, more easily or for less cost?

■ *SOCIABILITY* – Do I like to get on with people? Can I find ways to engage with a wide range of different types of people?

■ *COOPERATION* – Do I enjoy working together with other people to complete tasks and get results in a collaborative and inclusive way?

■ *EMPATHY* – Do I try to see another person's points of view and adapt my approach or goals in light of these so that we can both get something out of a situation?

■ *COMMUNICATION* – Can I speak and write clearly about things and can I persuade others to do *things that I see need to be done?*

- *ADAPTABILITY AND FLEXIBILITY – Can I change the way I do things when changing situations or circumstances mean that this is necessary to achieve the desired result?*

- *LEADERSHIP – Do you possess any leadership qualities? We once heard it said that one definition of leadership is 'getting someone else to follow you', so can you get other people to believe in you and your ideas and to help and support you through the challenges ahead?*

- *TENACITY – Do you have the resolve and drive to get through tough situations and not give up when it gets tough?*

This is a long list of personal attributes and it would be unusual for any single person to answer strongly 'yes' to all of these. But, in order to ascertain whether business ownership might be right for you, you should be able to tick off a good few of them. Ask people who are close to you, people you think know you well, to give you an honest appraisal as to which of these qualities they think that you possess.

If not, are there ways in which you could improve? Are you up for trying to develop in these areas? Alternatively, can you find others to work with who can provide some of the attributes to your business that you do not possess? Often two or more individuals do team up for this very reason – they are able to bring individual strengths that can compensate for each other. And if you truly do not possess a good measure of these personal characteristics, if you cannot develop them or work with others, then you should closely examine if this really is the right road for you.

Departure Point – Where Are You Coming From?

As we said earlier, there is no single 'right' place from which to start this journey. You are not too old, too young, too inexperienced or insufficiently qualified. It's never too early and it's not too late. You might be starting your journey from any number of different departure points. People often look to start working for themselves when they reach a transition point between different phases or crossroads in their lives. This can be one of a number of turbulent or uncomfortable events. In fact, a very large number of successful business owners cite 'overcoming adversity' as one of the main reasons why they got into their own business and why they were determined to succeed. Here are a few examples of some of these starting points, some of them seemingly inauspicious:

- *Leaving education to start work for the first time*
- *Retiring from employment but still with the energy and desire to do something else*
- *Being made redundant and determined to take control of your own destiny*
- *Currently working but looking for a fresh challenge*
- *Coming out of the care of the state (like care or the penal system) and seeking to stand on your own two feet*
- *Finishing an apprenticeship and looking to strike out on your own*
- *Looking to get back to work after a break but don't want to work for someone else*

Regardless of where you're coming from, the journey will be very similar. You may not be feeling too confident if you're going through transition but some of the best learning and personal growth often happens at difficult times. Let's now take a look in more detail at you as an individual and think about some of the personal motivations that are important in running your own business.

Your Motivation

We're probably all familiar with the famous quote usually attributed to the early twentieth-century mountaineer George Mallory. When asked why he chose to climb to the summit of Mount Everest,

Mallory replied 'Because it's there'. Sadly, Mallory met his demise while making an attempt at this goal but would at least have some satisfaction in securing immortality through his words and could pass on with the knowledge that at least he gave it a go.

In contrast to this sentiment, most people seldom give the same response if you ask them why they want to set and run their own business. And presumably most of them would wish to avoid a similar fate to Mr Mallory's, at least in the short term. As a would-be business owner reading this you will doubtless have some clear and specific motivations for pursuing this path. Typically, those who go it alone tend to start with the wish to want to make their living through their own business and a desire to take responsibility for themselves and what they do with their working life, rather than relying on others to provide them with a job and income.

The important thing is that you can feel the desire or motivation to want to set up and run your own business. You will need it because establishing a business is a big step and you should be thinking that you're in for the long haul so whatever your drive to do this you will need it to sustain you through the challenging times ahead.

When we run business start-up workshops with young people at Bright Ideas Trust, we always ask participants at the beginning to share with the group why they would want to own and run their own business. The answers are always very interesting and enlightening. Here are the six most common responses taken from the flipcharts we use in the session:

1   Make money

2   Make a difference to my family, community or society

3   Improve my life and lifestyle

4   Be my own boss and in control

5   Create a legacy

6   Gain self-fulfilment and personal satisfaction

So think about your motivation (or motivations) for becoming a business owner. Knowing this (or these) helps you to shape the type of business you want to create and to outline some clear goals so that you will know what you're aiming to achieve and when you've become successful. Here are a few things to think about when you're pondering your own drivers for wanting to do this.

1. Making money

Many people want to get into running their own business because it offers the opportunity to make money. Do you want to make a pile of money? A million? More? Or is this simply a way to earn a decent living for you and perhaps your family doing something that you really enjoy or something in which you think you can make a difference?

Some business people say that if you set out in business with the aim of just making money then you will fail. In one way they have a good point – it's more important to focus on providing customers with products and services that they want and need, building a fundamentally valuable business and enjoying the ride than simply trying to make money for yourself. If you do all these things, the money will follow anyway. But at the same time, you can do it purely for the money if you choose that route, although you will probably be forced to sacrifice other motivations and rewards if you go down this path.

When Paul was part of the management team that started Opta, a specialist business consultancy company, he and his fellow directors sat down in a hotel conference room near Gatwick airport for two days with a large whiteboard and a pack of multi-coloured dry-wipe pens. After a lot of debate (some of it strong) and much scribbling on the whiteboards, we eventually reached something of a consensus. We decided that whatever our business eventually did for its customers we would try to build a business that we could sell to another company through a trade sale within five years. So from the outset our aim, for better or worse, was to sell our business at some time in the future so that we would hopefully all become millionaires. Obviously our company would have to offer products and services that customers would want or need. But making a successful sale of our business as our primary aim informed just about all of the decisions that we made about the way in which we would design our business.

We'll return to whether or not we achieved this later but the important point was that we were clear that we were building a business that could be sold. Although some of us may have got enjoyment out of the type of work we did and made the most of the journey, the main motivation was to create a valuable business from which we could eventually realise the fruits of our labours.

This approach may not always provide you with some of the other things that you might want, such as having a personal life, flexibility or fun. If you're just making a dash for cash then you may be required to do things that you don't particularly enjoy doing and be forced to trade-off other things to achieve your goals. But it is an option.

2. Making a difference

By setting up and running your own business you will have the opportunity to make a difference. Do you want to help people through your business? For example, do you want to help or make a difference to your community or to society or to change the world? There are a growing number of people who want to start up their own business for this reason and in recent years we have seen the development of many 'social businesses' aimed at doing good things for society while at the same time making a profit. And there is no shame in these types of businesses making a profit. In fact, it's essential for them to continue in business, unless they aim to stay in business through donations (in which case they are not a true social business anyway).

When our friends at the *Big Issue* set up a radical new concept in publishing that enabled homeless people to take control of part of their lives by selling papers on the street, they were not thinking about getting rich. They wanted to help a group of underprivileged people to help themselves. The business would need to be profitable to be sustainable but this wasn't their primary motivation. They were social enterprise pioneers and have created something hugely worthwhile, but as individual founders they did not set out to, and have not, made a pile of money for themselves out of it.

Again, taking this approach to your business means that you may not be able to achieve others things that you might want. Typically social business owners do not earn as much as those seeking to make a return for their shareholders, although you may still need to work as hard to be successful.

3. Making a lifestyle change

Many people start their own business in order to change not just their job but also their way of life. Do you just want to create a better lifestyle for yourself with greater independence and flexibility in your working life? As we said, this is an important ambition for many starting a business. Most small businesses are most definitely in what is known as the 'lifestyle' category. That is to say, they are businesses that have been created by their owners in order to provide a livelihood and income for themselves as opposed to being aimed at being sold at some stage in the future.

When a friend of ours left her well-paid job as a manager at a leading mobile phone operator, she decided to set up her own business. She chose to create a business and personal coaching company to help people with personal development, work through career choices and deal with their personal issues and problems. From the outset she made it clear that she wanted three things – a business to provide her with a livelihood (no intention of building her business to sell it); a business that would allow her to use and enjoy using all her expertise in coaching people; and a way in which she would be able to spend more time with her young son. She was happy to work at weekends or in the evening from home. She did this and now works more hours than before, but when she chooses to work them. She's more productive and wastes less time because when she's at work she's always 100 per cent focused on working. But she turns down some work if it does not fit with her objectives – which means that she declines opportunities to make her business bigger and to earn more money.

4. Making myself boss

For many, running their own business offers them a chance to be in control of what they do at work every day without the constraints of having to do what their manager tells them. Is being your own boss with no one else telling you what you should and shouldn't do appealing to you? Having your own business is one way of gaining independence, freedom and control in your working life. Being your own boss can be liberating. There is no one to tell you what you should do and much freedom to take whatever course of action, what hours to work, how hard to work. But by the same token it will be up to you to see what needs to be done to make your business successful and then to make these things happen – if you do not do this then it will not get done and you will find it hard to succeed. So you need to take self-responsibility and to understand that the choices available and your actions will have consequences both good and not so good.

5. Creating a legacy

Creating a successful business that can be passed on to a family member can be a powerful motivator for many would-be business owners. It is worth considering what a legacy is. Traditionally, this is where you are looking to build something that you can leave behind or pass on to someone else in the future. But these days it's rare that 'Dombey Limited' becomes 'Dombey and Son' and is passed on to the next generation when the previous one retires. Often the younger generation does not want to take over. And many businesses fail within their first five years so your chances of creating something that will last long enough to pass on to someone else may be limited.

Another way of looking at the idea of legacy is to think about making the most of the journey and of taking out what you can along the way to pass on to others, rather than as an ultimate destination. An equally important consideration is that what you are doing by starting your own business is passing on a set of strong values about hard work, self-responsibility and trying to achieve something with your life.

6. Gaining self-fulfilment

And then there is the simple desire to gain some sort of personal non-financial reward from what you are doing through your business. Are you looking to gain a sense of self-fulfilment or simply personal satisfaction from running your own business? Many more people are now trying to gain satisfaction from their work as part of what has (tritely) become known as achieving a 'work–life balance'. Running your own business can certainly offer you opportunities to gain satisfaction – seeing your business grow as a result of your efforts, getting a thank you from a customer who really got what they wanted from you or simply watching your bank balance grow and knowing that you did that.

More than this, running your own business can allow you to personally develop and grow as a person in many ways. While some of the things that you will be required to do in the day-to-day course of events will be uncomfortable or even painful, achieving them can boost your self-confidence and move you to a higher level in terms of your sense of self-esteem. This can in turn help you in life more broadly with its daily challenges.

Working Hard

We once worked with a very successful sales director in a large firm who frequently said that he'd rather have a 'lucky' salesperson working in his team than a 'good' salesperson. He was right in some ways – getting a slice of luck can be hugely beneficial, particularly when the pressure's on. But as Gary Player, the champion South African golfer from years gone by, used to say, 'The more I practise, the luckier I get'. So, in business, never use the excuse that you were unlucky. No one will care about you being a victim of misfortune; only results matter. Don't submit to the urge to feel sorry for yourself and start bemoaning your luck. Keep believing that by your own persistence, determination and doing the right things you will make yourself some luck. Just about every successful person will tell you that they had some luck along the way. And almost all of them made this for themselves by doing the right things and by keeping going when they were less blessed. They made their own luck and so can you.

Courage and Determination

No matter who you are, what your experience or age, some measure of courage is required to take on the responsibility of running your own business. You are taking some risks, some real, some maybe imaginary. It's perfectly natural to feel some fear, uncertainty and doubt. If you don't then you should probably be asking yourself some serious questions about how much you care about what you are proposing to do. These thoughts and feelings can be used as drivers rather than inhibitors. You need to have a bit of anxiety to push you to make sure you succeed.

Why do you need courage and determination? Because when things are tough or going wrong it is usually only you who can put it right by keeping going. This takes courage. We are both long-distance runners and have completed many marathons. The thing that you always know after many miles when you're feeling exhausted is that in order to stop the pain all you have to do is . . . stop. But if you stop you will probably fail. The same applies with your business. And like running, if you can just get through the bad spell and keep going there is often a worthwhile payback at the end.

There's a good support network out there to help you along the road – there are all sorts of people who will be willing to assist you if you start to run into difficulties. And as long as you don't run up high levels of personal debts and ensure that you act within the law you can have as many goes at running your own business as you like. You can always try something else if it doesn't work out, providing that you try to learn from any mistakes you make along the way.

So, don't be put off because the prospect of starting out in the world of business is daunting or you feel slightly pessimistic at times or worry about whether or not you can be successful. The key is in the desire and the drive, wherever it comes from, to keep going and to prove that you can do it. There is no single personality type required to be successful in business, so don't be put off by what you read or see in the press or on television.

What's an Entrepreneur?

Many people want to start their own business but are put off because they don't think that they've got what it takes to be an Entrepreneur. Don't be put off by some of the commonly held beliefs about what you need to be an *entrepreneur*. What does the term entrepreneur actually mean anyway? These days the 'e' word is often abused and can cover a wide range of different things.

When we think of entrepreneurs we often think of wealthy tycoons who appear in the media and fly to meetings in their private jets, helicopters or chauffeur-driven limousines. The images conjured up are of multi-million pound business empires with fast cars, glass-plated office buildings and cohorts of attractive-looking staff. There is also a stereotypical personality of an entrepreneur – they are optimists, they are born leaders, they are extremely self-confident, they are charismatic, they inspire people, they have unquestioning self-belief. They are workaholics and have boundless energy. They can be highly self-assured to the point of arrogance. Some or all of this may be true. But this is often because the ones you see on the TV have usually already achieved a high degree of success – and many of them want to show you just how successful they have become!

More appropriately, an entrepreneur is generally someone who creates and owns a business enterprise and who is prepared to take personal responsibility and accountability for some level of personal, professional and/or financial risk to pursue their goals. The key words in this definition of an entrepreneur are:

- *Creates*
- *Business*
- *Responsibility*
- *Accountability*
- *Financial*
- *Risk*
- *Goals*

That's a definition, and in particular a set of individual words, that can equally apply to most small business owners. How many of them would use the 'e' word to describe themselves? Not many. For every 'entrepreneur' like this there are thousands of 'Business Owners' who are quietly running businesses that have a much lower profile but are no less valuable. Some of them are driven to become very rich (and some do) but many are content to achieve a decent living doing something for themselves, and those they are responsible for. Being a business owner may make you a millionaire – and if that's what you want then this is achievable in certain circumstances. But you don't only need to think of it in those terms because there are many other good reasons for wanting to run your own business.

We know plenty of people who have started up and built their own businesses who do not match the stereotypical description of an entrepreneur outlined above. Some of the best and most successful people we've worked with are sensitive, humble, self-deprecating, intelligent and introverted (the latter tend to listen more than extroverts, particularly to customers, which often makes them good salespeople).

It's also worth noting that the truly authentic entrepreneur tends to be at their most effective when starting a business. More often than not these individuals are prepared, and even eager, to hand over their baby to more appropriately qualified business managers once the venture is up and running so that they can move on to giving birth to their next idea. In reality being an entrepreneur is more of a mindset or a way of life than a career. So, let's dispel the myth that only 'entrepreneurs' can run businesses – someone who starts up and runs their own business should be thought of as a 'business owner' rather than an entrepreneur. And that's open to a wide range of different people.

So is business ownership for you? Our experience of working with hundreds of people over the last few years, many with little or no business experience but a desire to do this is . . . probably yes! Therefore, if you're still thinking that you could be right for business ownership, it's time to consider if it will be right for you. So what lies ahead if you choose this path?

WHAT LIES AHEAD?

'What lies behind us and what lies ahead of us are tiny matters compared to what lives within us.' Henry David Thoreau

Now that we have looked at whether you have the right qualities and motivation, we can look at some of the things that you will have to deal with if you run your own business. This section looks at whether business ownership will be right for you, exploring some of the pros and cons of running your own business and looking at what it might be like for you if you choose to go on this journey. It goes on to outline what you can expect to get involved with in your day-to-day business life.

Is Business Ownership Right for Me?

Before setting out on this journey it's important to think long and hard about what this might be like. Forewarned is forearmed. Owning your own business is a serious undertaking. You are proposing to become wedded to your business, for better or for worse, potentially for a long time. There will be many ups and downs over that time so making sure that you and running your own business are well matched to each other is an important first step.

It's a fact that running a business is not for everyone. If, as a result of reading this or looking into what's involved more generally, you decide that it's not for you then that will not be so bad a thing. So, will having my own business be right for me? And what will it be like? As with most things in life, business ownership has its pros and cons. Take these on board before you set off. The good news is that starting up your own business can be rewarding in many ways and can offer you some fantastic advantages over working for someone else. But there are some downsides too – if you choose this way of life you will not be able to avoid them entirely – so make sure that you think you can cope with them.

Some pros

1   **Financial Independence** – There can be attractive financial rewards both during and at the end of the journey. The amount that you can earn from your business is, at least theoretically, unlimited. There is no boss to tell you that you can't have a pay rise this year, except yourself of course. If your business does well you will have the opportunity to personally reap the financial rewards from your labours, rather than see this go to those that you work for or to shareholders sitting far away

2   **Freedom** – It can give you independence, a greater degree of personal freedom and allow you to be your own boss. This is one of the main drivers for a large number of small business owners, much more so than the potential financial rewards that can be gained

3   **Take the Challenge** – It's a great personal challenge – one that will ask many questions of you and test you to the limits of

where you thought you could go. You will be required to make many decisions, some of which may involve uncomfortable choices and which will have a real impact on your life and the lives of others. You will have to live with the consequences of those decisions. But the rewards of going through this can be huge and many who follow this path report that they developed as individuals greatly and enjoyed the process at the same time

4   **Change of Life** – It can change your lifestyle by giving you flexibility in the way that you work. For example, being able to work at or near your home (or away from home if that's what you prefer) and the hours that suit you best

5   **Helping Hands** – It can give you a real chance to make a difference – to other people's lives, your community, your family and yourself. This is becoming increasingly important to people. Over the last few years there has been a steep rise in interest in setting up businesses aiming to do this and more and more people are seeking to do more than just try to maximise their profits

6   **Personal Development** – It's a fantastic learning experience. We once heard setting up and running your own business was like doing an on-the-job, practical Masters in Business Administration (MBA) – except that it was useful at the same time!

7   **Business or Pleasure** – It can be enormous fun. Most people who follow the business ownership path will tell you that while it can be very demanding and challenging, there are fun times along the way. Everyone that's owned their own business can tell you about some of the funny experiences (usually not that funny at the time) that they've had along the way

. . . and some cons

Running your own business can have a number of downsides and some potential pitfalls – if you don't take a few of the necessary steps to protect yourself it can lead to a painful experience. We make no apologies for placing emphasis on this, even if it appears slightly off-putting or might discourage you. It's much better to be fully aware of the disadvantages of running your own business before you take the plunge. It's really not for everyone; so go in with your eyes open.

1   **Long Haul** – If you're really serious about starting a business you need to be prepared to be in it for the long haul. Like a new pet, it's not just for Christmas. Think of it in terms of taking about 1,000 days to get properly established. Only after this time will you have a clearer view about whether you are succeeding or not and how your business will really work out over the long term. Rarely are people able to build up a successful, sustainable business inside this three-year period and it's often only after this length of time that you will be able to start reaping the financial fruits of your labours. Until then you'll probably still be investing or reinvesting anything that you make and not expecting to be taking much out of the business for yourself. In businesses that we've built up with the intention of seeking to sell them on, it's typically taken us five–seven years to create something attractive to that purchaser. It takes time to get started, build up customers, make some mistakes, recover, achieve growth, keep all the plates spinning, refine or completely change what you offer your customers as the market you're in moves on (which it does all the time) and have enough consistently good performance to be financially sustainable or to persuade a potential acquirer of your business that you're what they're looking for

2   **High Work Rate** – There's a lot of hard work to do. You will hear business owners say this a lot and they are not exaggerating. In business the saying that it's 1 per cent inspiration and 99 per cent perspiration is highly applicable. You will find yourself having to do everything from cold calling customers to handing out flyers and assembling office furniture to making the IT work

3   **Loneliness** – It can get lonely, there can be heartache and anger and apprehension. You may find yourself waking up in the middle of the night worrying about how you are going to pay a bill or where your next sale is coming from. If you think that the idea of you nursing a cup of tea in the early hours while you wrestle with the problem sounds rather romantic, forget it – it's not nice. You may have to make some difficult decisions – there

will be hard choices to be made and when that happens there is always anxiety

4   **Stuff Happens** – There are the tough times – when you lose an important customer, some equipment breaks down or a key member of staff fails to turn up to work. You may need to put up with customers that you don't like or might have to beg, borrow or make do. You must be able to deal with these sorts of things. And, there will be many times when you simply don't know what you're doing and have to admit to it, and try to find a solution to the problem at hand

5   **Just You** – Remember we said that being your own boss could give you greater freedom? While this can be true, it tends to be a different kind of freedom. Many of the young people that we work with at Bright Ideas Trust report that they actually have less personal freedom than they did before they started in their own business. Because freedom is not free. The difference is that if you run your own business you are free from the constraints of working for someone else. But often nothing gets done unless you do it so there are times when you can feel like you're all on your own

6   **Tripping Up** – And then you will make some mistakes, probably many mistakes – anyone that tries to tell you that you will not do this is deluded or being untruthful. And these will cost you. Anyone that tells you that all you have to do is just follow their advice, or the way they did it (or even their book!) and you will not make these mistakes, is doing likewise. Making mistakes is an important part of making the journey a rewarding one. The important thing is to recognise and learn from the mistakes. By doing this you will gain huge satisfaction from the next time you do it right and realise that you have personally grown and developed

7   **Going Without** – And your business may not provide you with the riches that you were dreaming of making. In fact, for some period of time it may not provide you with anything at all. If the business doesn't generate the income required to cover its costs with something left over it will almost certainly be *you* who will be earning no salary or wages that week or month. So you may have to make do with less than you thought or would like. And

this means that you will need to make sure that you can meet your financial commitments, like paying the mortgage or rent, keeping the lights on and food, for any period of time when the business cannot afford to pay you

There should be no doubt in the mind of the wannabe business owner that there are drawbacks and they need to be clearly spelt out. But the truth is that the upsides are far greater if this is the life for you. Most who start up and run their own business find that the sense of personal freedom and the satisfaction gained from getting results far outweigh the disadvantages. They will tell you that although it can be far harder work than being an employee of someone else, it's much more rewarding in all sorts of ways and that they are happy to take on the multitude of challenges. And everyone we know that has gone down this road cannot conceive of going back to work for someone else again.

Risks and Rewards

Anyone who starts his or her own business is taking a risk. The amount and type of risk will vary, but there's always some form of risk. There is a clear and simple logic behind this equation, but are you ready for it? Usually people are prepared to take the risk in the hope of generating some sort of reward, either financial, lifestyle-based or through being more socially responsible, which is greater than the reward that they would have gained had they not taken that risk. You could get a job working for someone else with little risk, but this might give you limited rewards. But you may want to take a bigger risk to get greater reward. In this quest you might succeed, but by the same token you might fail.

It's not a disaster if your business fails – you will almost certainly learn many things along the way. In recent times we have as a society become perhaps too preoccupied with minimising risks and trying to avoid failure, but it is hard to see how the human race would have developed over millennia without taking risks and experiencing a mixture of success and failure as a result. This is a key factor in how we have learned and thrived as a species.

If you fail, be assured that you can dust yourself down and start again. But this is only half of the story because in many ways you will not really have failed anyway because you should have learned a lot of lessons that will serve you well the next time. And some of the things that you have learned can be taken and used in your next attempt. It has been well-documented that Bebo was Paul Birch's sixth attempt at starting a business – three were complete failures, two moderate successes and the sixth was Bebo.

The failures are the scars that every successful business owner has, including many of the most famous and successful. It is said that Henry Ford, the initiator of mass production, became bankrupt five times before he finally established the successful and very long-running Ford Motor Company. And Bill Gates, having dropped out of university, initially set up a business called Traf-O-Data with Paul Allen, his eventual co-founder of Microsoft. This first effort failed . . . but needless to say that the second did not.

Life in a Day

So what's an average day in the life of a business owner? This will vary depending upon the type of business that you intend to start, what your role in it will be, if you have staff, how big you want to grow to and so on. However, business ownership will always mean that you will be regularly involved with some or all of the following set of things – so are you up for spending your days doing these kinds of activities?

- ■ *SALES – Selling to customers – including making sales presentations, negotiating sales, putting proposals and quotes together*

- ■ *CUSTOMER SERVICE – Managing customers – including delivering your product or service, invoicing, dealing with queries and complaints and chasing for payments*

- ■ *FINANCIAL – Managing day-to-day financial matters – including keeping track of VAT receipts and payments, preparing invoices and dealing with your accountant*

- *SUPPLIERS* – Managing suppliers – including negotiating contracts, sorting out problems, such as late deliveries or faulty goods

- *STAFF* – Managing staff issues – including recruiting, negotiating terms of employment, employment contracts, training on the job, dealing with discipline, grievance problems and dismissal procedures

- *IT* – Procuring and making your IT and computing work properly

- *ADMINISTRATION* – Keeping good records, filing, dealing with government bodies, such as HMRC and Companies House

Your immediate reaction to this list might be that you either do not or cannot do some of these things. This is fine at this stage but the important thing is to be ready and willing to engage with and take an interest in them as you go forward. Even if you ultimately get others to do some of these types of essential business activities, be prepared to take an interest in all of them to some extent because in the end it will be you who is responsible for making sure that they get done and to the standard that you would want.

Of course, this list excludes actually making your product or delivering your service, which is obviously central to your business, so you will need to have enough time to do that as well! Most business owners will tell you that there are never enough hours in the day and that there is always something more to do. And at times you can expect to be working late into the evening and sacrificing other things in your life. But keep in mind that all your hard work will be worth it.

THINKING IT THROUGH

WHAT'S YOUR BRIGHT IDEA?

'Ideas are the beginning points
of all fortunes.' Napoleon Hill

Now you're probably straining at the leash to get on
with your idea but we had to take you on that little
detour first so that you think hard about why you're
doing this and if you're right for it. Now we move
on to talk about ideas for what your business will be
all about. Whether you already have a bright idea or
are in need of some inspiration, this chapter provides
some ways in which you could look for business ideas
and describes some of the different goals that you
might consider for your business.

Where Are You Going?

There's an old saying that business is the 'conversion of market opportunity into cash in the bank'. That's fine, except that it conveniently omits to mention anything about the rather important bit in the middle – your business idea: the idea that will get you from the market opportunity starting line to the cash in the bank finishing post. We've already looked at you and where you are coming from in the previous chapter. Now we need to move on to looking at where you want to get to and your business idea.

Although you may think that everyone in business is trying to achieve the same aim, in reality there are different destinations. At the outset, think for a while about where you might be trying to get to if you have your own business. It's probably one of the following:

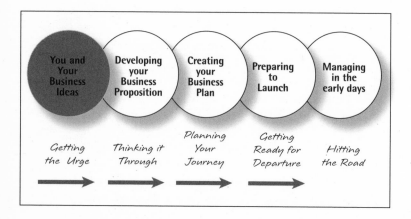

Lifestyle business

Lifestyle businesses are set up and run by their owners primarily with the aim of supporting and enhancing their lifestyle. The motivation of this type of business owner tends to revolve around independence, flexibility, being their own boss and doing what they enjoy doing at work. These types of businesses typically rely on the founders' skills, personality, energy and network of contacts. Many of them are one-person services businesses, like consultancy and trades or as retailers. Success for them is often measured by an increase in satisfaction with their owner's overall life quality rather than simply making a pile of money.

Some types of businesses are less accessible than others to the would-be lifestyle business owner. Typically, those requiring large amounts of start-up capital are difficult to launch and sustain on a lifestyle basis – imagine trying to set up a car manufacturing plant, launch a new perfume brand or start producing computers. But many others, such as small creative industry businesses, service companies and stores are highly attractive for individual business owners or small groups.

Lifestyle businesses typically have limited potential for large growth because this will often alter the lifestyle for which their owner has set them up. External financial investors rarely get involved with lifestyle businesses because of this lack of scalability but this does not mean that lifestyle businesses are not worthwhile. On the contrary, a large proportion of all small businesses are run on this basis and provide outstanding products and services for their customers and give fulfilling occupations (and lifestyles) for their owners.

Equity or exit-driven business

An equity or exit-driven business is one where the owner or owners intentionally set out to create a business as an asset with real value so that it can be sold – either partially or as an entire business – to others in return for a significant gain. The sale of the business will typically be to another company (through a trade sale or by merging with another company) or to individuals and financial institutions (through being floated on a public market, like the FTSE or AIM markets). Success can be defined as the increase in value of the business over time and ultimately in that the business is sold, yielding a return for its owners.

Equity businesses typically have the ability to reach a significant scale and will be able to achieve this without a reliance on the owners delivering everything. In other words, they will exist in a relatively large market and be able to replicate what they do in order to grow. Often they will be built with the support of funding from external investors (such as venture capital companies or business angels) who are motivated to achieve a return on this investment of many times their initial outlay. Equity businesses cannot be reliant on the individual skills, knowledge or experience of one person, since this is not scalable – a single person can only be in one place at one time and so to expand they need to assemble a team of complementary individuals to work together.

Social business

Social businesses aim to do good for others in their community or society. The main difference between social businesses and other businesses is that the profits from these types of ventures are intended be ploughed back into the business rather than going into the pockets of the owners or shareholders for personal gain. Social businesses tend to set up as mutual or cooperative societies (like the building societies before they changed into banks, or The Coop) or as charities and companies limited by guarantee.

Even though social business has been around for decades, there remains some confusion about the actual definition of this type of business. Too much is made of this – social businesses are really like any other form of commercial business except they have a clear mission to primarily do something worthwhile beyond simply making a return for their shareholders. But it's critical that they do make a profit too in order that they can be self-sustaining rather than relying on donations to keep them going. The key difference between a true social business and one that is not is that any profits made will always be reinvested back into the business and not taken out by the owners.

Mixing it up

You can actually try to do a combination of a lifestyle business and an equity-driven business if you are so inclined. You may not have a single destination when you start out – many begin by aiming to run their own business to support their lifestyle but change track to an equity-type business later. Whichever way you go, you need to make sure that you are trying to create a fundamentally sound business. This means that you are aiming to build something that has real customers who pay you for the products and services that you sell them and where you are making more money than you are spending. Whether Lifestyle or Equity or Social, this is a fundamental decision that you need to make when you're thinking through how your business is going to work. Neither is good or bad. It's just a question of which one is for you.

What's Your Bright Idea?

If you've got an idea of where you want to go then that's great but if you haven't then you need to find the inspiration for your business idea. It doesn't need to be the next iPad or must-use social network. It can be anything you like as long as you can be enthusiastic about it, that it will satisfy a customer need and you think it can make money.

We've seen many people succeed with new businesses that provided very similar products and services to existing companies in the market. But they found a better way to do it than their competitors. We've also seen many 'best things since sliced bread' ideas completely fail, usually because they weren't thought through properly or the implementation and operation of the business was poorly managed. So when you are seeking inspiration for your business idea, what should you look for?

1. Meeting a need

It's very important to grasp that whatever you choose to offer your customers, they will not buy it from you unless it meets some sort of need that they have. Try to think of business ideas where you can clearly see that there is a customer need, or if you have an idea already, whether it passes this test.

As a keen musician and member of a band, Ben Walters became increasingly frustrated that he could not get access to the standard of rehearsal and recording studio facilities that he wanted. There were hardly any facilities within thirty miles of his home and those that there were offered worn-out equipment, rooms that were too small, little support and assistance, no on-site expertise and poor customer service. As a musician he had a good idea of what other musicians need. So he came to us at Bright Ideas Trust with a plan to create a modern, well-equipped and maintained recording and rehearsal facility that would offer customers a high level of customer service at affordable rates. Audium Recording & Production is now up and running in south-east London.

Sean Brown set up his cleaning business to cater for the needs of estate agents looking to have rental properties cleaned prior to a new tenant taking over. Sean saw a gap in the market because he was working as an estate agent and realised that this need was not being well served by any other cleaning business in his area. As a result of doing this he felt more certain that there would be a market and he gained a large amount of confidence that he would be able to execute his strategy. He also learned the most efficient way to operate and while thinking it through discovered that there were many other needs he could meet with commercial customers that needed office-cleaning services. So he left the estate agents and set up his rent-a-cleaner business to take advantage of this opportunity and has been successful ever since.

2. Know your onions

Focus on things that you know about. The first rule for a budding novelist is said to be to write about things that they know about. The same goes for business. Whatever you choose to do, you should pick an area that you know something, and preferably quite a lot, about. Many successful business people say that they got into a particular field because not only did they know something about it, but also they were passionate about it. And this passion for your product, service or industry will carry you through the trials and tribulations of getting established in business. You will almost certainly be competing against people who know about the industry and the market you're operating in so you'd better be at least the equal of your competitors in this respect from the start or find a way to get there quickly after you start.

When Fabien Souzandry set up v.ographics limited, a small film production company making short films for the business community, he had already spent several years working with other film producers. Over the course of a few years he was able to take on small pieces of work as a subcontractor or as a volunteer and to train on the job. He saw this time as an investment in his future business and learned much of what was required to enable him to start his own company. He operates in a highly competitive business with many suppliers but his passion, commitment and knowledge of the industry make him successful. He is now not only making promotional films for companies but has worked on a film that was nominated for an award at the Cannes Film Festival.

In Fabien's case, when he started his business he had already acquired the knowledge, skills and experience of working in his particular industry so that he could utilise this to the benefit of his new business.

3. All change

It's often useful to look for business opportunities where there are changes happening or predicted to happen in the near future. These changes will almost certainly generate one or more needs for a potential customer somewhere. Examples of the types of changes that take place include:

- *New technology introduction*
- *Changes in society or community*
- *New laws or regulations*
- *Trends in consumer attitudes or tastes*
- *. . . or some other change*

When the UK government introduced the Road Safety Act 2006, not many people would have thought about this being a great business opportunity. Ordinarily this event would go unnoticed by all but the most ardent anorak-wearing follower of government business and of course some lawyers and the police. Actually more people should have been interested in this because it brought in new penalties for speeding so it became easier to lose your driving licence. Since its introduction, some people have collected enough penalty points to lose their licence in a single day! This change creates a 'point of pain' for some people – and a need to deal with that pain.

We invested in a business that came up with a solution to meet this need and potentially salve the pain. They created the technology to link up several existing databases of information which showed the location of every speed camera in the UK, integrated this information with the software in a standard GPS-based mapping system and reported this through a satellite navigation device in the car, giving fair warning to drivers – and in a legal way. The people who started this business saw the change, recognised that this change would create a problem or a need for thousands of people and created something to meet this need. Today, this business is thriving and anyone buying a leading brand of satellite navigation device will probably find its technology embedded in their system and ready to work as soon as they switch it on.

4. Size matters

Unless you have good reasons to go for something really ambitious with thoughts of creating a company worth millions of pounds, keep it small to start with. Get going with something manageable and realistic, particularly if this is your first venture. Give yourself the chance to learn what you are doing, make some mistakes, correct them and become successful before you try to expand too quickly. The temptation is to try to run before you can walk and this can lead to making errors that can be both financially and emotionally costly and can give your self-confidence a real knock. Furthermore, larger businesses typically require larger amounts of capital investment to get them going and unless you have a track record of building successful businesses this will be very difficult to obtain from the sorts of external investors that you would need to go to. So give yourself some breathing space so that you don't set yourself unrealistic expectations that you will probably fail to meet and, by doing so, subject yourself to unnecessary discouragement. Alan Sugar started the Amstrad empire by selling boiled beetroot from the back of his van on a local market before expanding into other areas. Start small – you can always take it global next year!

5. . . . and now for something NOT completely different

If we had a fiver for everyone that we've heard say, 'I'd love to have my own business, all I need is an idea,' we'd be far away on a Caribbean beach by now swaying gently in our hammock while sipping something cool and amber. So where do you get the inspiration?

For some people this is very easy. They may have dreamed of doing a particular thing since childhood or they're hit by a 'bolt from the blue' one day and just know what they have to do. Or some life-changing event takes place and drives them down a particular road. And then there are the rest of us, to whom this does not happen. Many seem to think that you need to do something truly unique, world changing, awe inspiring or never done before in order to be successful in business. But this could not be further from the truth. So what should we do?

Do something *similar* to that which is already being done in the market place, particularly if it's your first attempt at running your own business. The majority of businesses in the world offer similar products or services to many other businesses – how many taxi companies are there in your local area? Wherever you live, you can generally find more than one of most types of business – how many hairdressers or builders or restaurants or photographers or music teachers are there in your area? The existing players have already proved that there is a market and there are customers spending money on them.

The crucial point is that if you choose to do something similar to others already out there, make sure that your product or service is seen by your customers as being in some way different from what they can already buy and will meet their needs better.

Will King launched King of Shaves, a range of shaving and skincare products, in 1993 against massive existing competition from many household name brands, like Gillette, with enormous marketing budgets. He created a shaving oil that eased the pain, rash and burn that the founder had experienced during shaving. So his idea was to try to offer a set of products that better met the needs of a particular group of shaving customers who were not able to get what they needed from existing providers, but in a well-established and highly competitive market. In 2008 King of Shaves had sales of around £25m, proving it is possible.

There is and always will be room for new companies to get into existing markets, even those that are seemingly saturated with heavyweight competitors who appear untouchable. But you do need to find a convincing way to do it better for the customers of those products and services than those already available.

6. Inflamed passions

Maybe your inspiration will spring from something that infuriates you because you can just see that it could be done better or you can't quite get want you want. We've all been the recipient of bad service, faulty products or frustrating customer services. We've all thought that what's available in the market is just too expensive and should be cheaper. So why not use this irritation to drive you to do something about it and to do it better than what is currently available in your market? Alternatively, do something that you care deeply about and want to make a difference to – this is often a strong motivator for people setting up social businesses.

When James Murray-Wells was a student he was told that he needed glasses but was shocked to discover that they cost so much – as someone on a low income he could not afford something that was so important to him. He started looking at the real cost of making a pair of reading glasses and decided that he would try to sell them via the web. Glasses Direct started in 2004 and today has a multimillion-pound turnover.

Will My Idea Work?

How can you tell if your idea is any good or not, or if it will work in the market, or if anyone will buy from you, or if you will be able to make money from it, or if you're just plain crazy? This is, of course, the $64,000 question and one that can rarely, if ever, be answered until you give it a go. Some of the greatest business ideas ever thought of have been turned down by apparently intelligent people as having no chance; conversely, what good judges consider to be sure-fire winners can go on to fail.

So if we cannot know the answer now, we can at least take the next steps on the journey to try to get closer to establishing whether or not your proposition might work. We would suggest that there are two next logical steps on your journey:

- Find an experienced business person to act as your business mentor and help you to answer some of these questions

- Think it through properly, preferably with your mentor, so that you don't go charging off in wrong directions potentially causing yourself a lot of heartache later

We turn now to more detail on the importance of *business mentoring* (Chapter 5) and the power of *thinking it through thoroughly* (Chapter 6).

GETTING GUIDANCE

'Mentor: someone whose hindsight can become your foresight.'

So you have a business idea. Now in this chapter we discuss finding an experienced business person to help you develop your idea into a sound Business Proposition. Finding yourself a business mentor is the most important help that you can look for. We also describe some of the other types of assistance you should consider.

Helping Hands

When Sigmund Freud put forward the notion of being 'in denial' he probably wasn't thinking about people starting their own business. He used this phrase to describe the situation where an individual, faced with facts that are too uncomfortable to accept, will reject them in spite of clear evidence to the contrary. We probably all know someone who at some time or another has acted like this. Sometimes people spend much of their lives in this state and it's usually not a good place to be because it can lead to poor judgement, wrong decisions and the tendency to treat those around you badly.

If being in denial is not a good place to be in life then it's a particularly bad position to get into in business. The commercial world will typically be harsh on all but a few who are not alert and aware of what they are doing and what is really happening around them or who do not listen, observe and learn. You must be in touch with what's going on around you – your customers, the market and your competition – to be successful.

But the truth is that as someone starting out on your first business (or for that matter your one hundred and first) you will not know everything required about how to do this. Wrongly believing that you know best and being even the slightest bit arrogant about this can be dangerous because it can often lead to you being punished by the hard commercial world. A good first step when you're thinking about starting your business, therefore, is to admit that you don't know it all (believe us, you don't) and to get someone with some experience to help you, both with your thinking it through, your planning and everything that follows.

Getting Help

One person in isolation rarely creates businesses. Not many successful businesses anyway. You can of course share your ideas and plans with your parents, friends, teacher or complete strangers with no background in creating a business, but this will only take you so far. At some point you will be well advised to connect with someone who has some experience of running their own business to help you out. This is your Business Mentor.

When we work with people who are looking to start their own business there is one thing that they all tell us they need above all other things – and this includes money. They say that they would like to get the help of someone who has experience of starting up and developing a small business and who is willing to pass this knowledge on to them in ways that they can understand.

This request does not just apply to business virgins, but also to entrepreneurs with experience of working with venture capital companies who are approached by businesses looking for millions of pounds of funding. Typically, the experienced people who run these businesses say that they want to work with venture capital companies that will give them help and support beyond just the cash injection. They are usually looking for a financial backer who will also provide them with know-how, skills and experience to help them expand their venture. So if really experienced business managers need it, then those starting out on this journey almost certainly do as well. So, find yourself a Business Mentor to help you with this.

It is important to take this step sooner rather than later in your journey. Start talking with someone who has been down this road in the past as soon as you think that you want to set up your own business and have some ideas about what you want to do. This means before you get into the detail of working out your business plan and certainly before you start spending money or launching into the market. There is much thinking to do before you get to those stages and you will save yourself time and money by pausing and seeking advice before potentially embarking upon a flawed business idea.

What is a Mentor?

Your mentor is someone who wants to help you to develop your business. They must have a desire to want to pass on the knowledge that they have acquired by running their own business. They might call it 'giving something back' but you can also think of it as part of the great human tradition of 'passing something on' to the next generation.

Your mentor is someone who will believe in you and understands and sees merit in your business idea – they 'get it', so to speak. They will offer practical, commonsense suggestions and solutions to help you to solve the myriad of problems that you will face every day as you plan, launch and run your business. They can help to guide you down the right path for your business and away from the sometimes tempting but potentially wrong turnings that you could take, as well as provide you personally with focus, direction and support. They will only be able to offer this if they have experienced similar situations to those that you will find yourself in.

Your mentor is someone that you can trust. Building this trust may take a while, but over time you will need to build a relationship based on open and honest communication – if you have the tendency to withhold bad news or information about things you might be embarrassed to admit to then forget that – they will need you to be open so that they can help you. They are not your parent or a teacher waiting patiently to scold you – they are there to support you even if you've made an embarrassing mistake that you don't want to admit to. Unless you get all the cards on the table a solution cannot be found to a problem. It takes time and probably changes over the course of time, but this can be a powerful and rewarding relationship for both you as the mentee and your mentor.

Mentor Experience

Business Mentors can come from a wide range of backgrounds. However, whatever else they have, they should be someone who has got experience of setting up and running their own business. Ideally they will also be someone who has done this from scratch. They may also have sold their business to another person or company, which will give them a valuable insight into how this process goes and what's important to an acquirer so that you can build this into your plans from the start. Do not settle for someone who has not got the experience of having run their own business, because without it they may be extremely worthy and well meaning (good in itself) but they will not have what you need.

This experience will often come with many years of working in their own business. But many younger business owners are becoming more interested in passing on their experience to the next generation and this is good. It's not essential that you find someone who was successful thirty years ago and is now in semi-retirement and has the time to do this. Finding a mentor who is still very active and only a few years ahead of you can be really good. From our experience of this these mentors say that they gain a great deal out of this to take back to their businesses as well. It's sometimes said that the best way to learn something is to teach it, and this would seem to be a good case in point.

How Do You Do It?

There is no set way to make the relationship with your mentor work well. It's whatever works for you both. The mentor should try to help you identify the best approach for you but you need to agree about it.

Your mentor should be listening very carefully to you and trying to understand you as a person – what your motivations are, how you learn best, your way of working, how to get the best out of you – as well as what you are trying to achieve with the business. If they do the former they will get a much better idea of how to help you.

You should try to meet regularly. Ideally you should both prepare an agenda that you want to cover when you meet. This will save you time at the beginning, but you might also find that taking a few minutes at the start to just talk about what's been happening and then let an agenda form out of that conversation an equally good use of time. Either way, take the approach where the emphasis is on you to be proactive and take the initiative, so be prepared – make the most of the time that they are giving you. Don't expect your mentor to do all the work, even if you are slightly in awe of their greater knowledge and expertise; they will appreciate it if you prepare and are on the front foot, even if you don't always get it right. If they are worth their salt, they will not laugh at you, we promise. Again, good business mentors appreciate people who make the effort – these are the types of people that they want to hire for their companies so it's what they're looking for.

When you meet start by looking at the big picture, then break things down into detail – both the devil and the delight are in the detail. Always conclude your meetings with some sort of action plan and with some clear goals. Make this clear, concrete and practical: focus on what you need to do to develop your business between now and the next time you sit down together. Your mentor should be seeking to stretch you to a point where you are really challenged but not to the point of breaking. Don't be afraid of being pushed: you should be seeking this not shirking it, although also do negotiate what you think is realistic – this is good practice anyway for your business dealings in general.

Your mentor should challenge, encourage, cajole and sympathise. They can be a shoulder to cry on and an outlet for your frustrations. A problem shared truly can often be a problem halved. Your mentor can help you to see what needs to be done, set targets for you and challenge you to do it. So it's about giving you time, helping you to see what needs to be done or how to solve a problem, sometimes showing you what needs to be done, really caring and not just playing at it in order to impress people, doing whatever it takes, doing it alongside you if required and being prepared to take on some tasks to help you along the way.

What's in it for the Mentor?

It's important to consider why people would want to be your mentor in the first place – thinking about this from the other person's viewpoint can also help you to get the most out of the relationship. Remember, it's their life too.

Mentoring, giving something back, passing something on, whatever you want to call it, has developed over the last few years. Many more people are now becoming more interested in being successful through virtue and doing something to help others rather than pursuing pure self-interest. The days of the 'me' generation are hopefully beginning to draw to a close and there is a greater willingness to try to support the development of others, particularly the next generation of business people.

Your mentor may be doing this altruistically, happy to pass on their knowledge without reward, but if we're completely honest about it they will need to gain something for themselves. This may be as simple as gaining the personal satisfaction of having helped someone else to achieve their dream or learning new things from you about what's going on in the world.

Should I Pay for a Mentor?

This is a debatable point. Many potential mentors will offer to help you for nothing, but some individuals and a number of organisations do charge for this as a service. Clearly there can be great value in it, and as budding business people, you should not fail to recognise that with value comes a price – you will not be looking to give away for free the service you offer to your customers. However, your starting point should be to find someone suitable who is willing to be your mentor on a 'pro bono' basis, that is to say, free of charge. Mentors will know that in the early stages of getting your business off the ground you should be trying to conserve your cash and they will not want to put an additional burden on your costs. When we started this type of relationship a few years ago it was done on a free-of-charge basis . . . but Tim usually bought the lunch!

Where Do I Find My Mentor?

Do you know someone like this? Probably not, but don't despair. There are people who can help you with this. In recent years a number of organisations have sprung up that can provide a sort of dating agency for business owners and mentors. At Bright Ideas Trust we are promoting this change through our mentoring programme, which we are making one of the best in the country. Many other fine organisations also exist to help you with this – you can go to find a current list of places to look for a mentor at www.whatsyourbright idea.biz and take a look.

Some Dos of Mentoring

1   **Joint Endeavour** – Both you and your mentor must decide that you want to engage in this relationship or it will not work properly. Mentoring is a two-way street – you must want them to be your mentor *and* they must want to mentor you. There must be something in it for both of you

2   **Time Commitment** – Your mentor must have enough time to

help you and be prepared to give you as much as you need. Some people need merely a telephone call once a week to chat things through, and a few email exchanges. Some need a weekly face-to-face meeting as well. Often the amount of help varies through time or as issues arise. There is no set formula, but it's important to agree with your mentor what you both need from the relationship. Overall, we would recommend that you are demanding of your mentor and ask them for what you want. If they can't do it they will tell you so. You should be able to reach a mutually acceptable arrangement. Good mentors are busy people so you should expect them to be straight with you about what time they can commit

3   **Arm's Length** – Mentors should not invest money in your business and should not be involved in day-to-day executive activities. They can invest as much time in you as you agree, but not cash. They need to be objective and 100 per cent in there for you. If they want a stake in your business or to lend you money they can be a shareholder or a director or a creditor, but find someone else to be your mentor

4   **Only Us** – Many people who have made the mentor/mentee relationship work well for them report that having more than one mentor can work well. But in most cases a single mentor with whom you can develop a close and personal relationship works best at any point in time

5   **Action Plan** – Set objectives and agree an action plan at the conclusion of each meeting. Typically, small business people have no one to hold them to account – that's one of the reasons why you did this, wasn't it, so that you could do whatever you wanted? But it helps a lot to have someone asking difficult questions of you, albeit in a supportive and safe way

6   **Experience Counts** – General business or life coaches will not do – you need an experienced business person who at times might need to give you clear and direct instructions about what you need to do to deal with a particular situation

7   **Have a Conversation** – A large part of the mentor/mentee relationship is just that – a relationship. So spend some time just talking about what's working and what isn't. Ask how we

are doing in terms of the relationship, the learning process for both of you as well as assessing progress in achieving your business objectives

8   **Research Each Other** – Find out about each other in advance if you can. If a third party introduced you, ask them to give you some background. Make sure that you think you have someone who is right for you before you meet and do your preparation – you will get off to a much better start. Tim met with a few potential mentors before he started to work with Paul

9   **Reward and Recognition** – Make sure that you give your mentor good feedback on how you think things are working. Don't be shy about giving them praise when you think that they have helped you and make suggestions about how you think the arrangement could be improved

10 **Patience** – Finding a good mentor may not be easy: to find someone with the right experience, temperament and inclination to suit you may take time

BUSINESS PROPOSITION

'No problem can withstand the assault of sustained thinking.'
Voltaire

In the last section we talked about the power of mentoring and how a good mentor can help you develop your business. Now we move on to explain the concept of the Business Proposition and show the importance of carefully thinking through your proposition before you go too much further. We provide a simple framework to use to develop your Business Proposition and guidance on how to do this.

What's a Business Proposition?

Now that you've spent some time thinking about yourself, your business idea and how to get some help, it's time to turn to how you move forward. There is no single 'right' way to do this but before you dive headlong into launching your great new business concept on an unsuspecting public there are a few basic stepping stones that need to be followed if you want to make it. Starting with thinking through properly what you are going to do. Looking before leaping. We're going to come on to some ways in which you can structure and arrange your thinking to help you get the most out of it.

There is not much business jargon in this book. But the term Business Proposition is one phrase that we make no apologies for using. It's one of the most important things that you are going to do in the course of creating your business. Your Business Proposition is simply a description of what your business is going to do. From our years of experience of designing and launching new businesses, products and services, we recommend that you invest time and effort in this. It gives you a straightforward process by which to clearly describe what your business does for its customers by looking at it principally from their point of view.

Business Proposition in Context

Once you have decided on your business idea, this is the next step to take on the journey to starting your business. Do this before you start to write a business plan – once you are more convinced in your own mind that you have something worth developing then take the time and effort to write this into a plan. Your Business Proposition and Business Plan are very different things and it is important to understand the difference between the two. Your Business Proposition is a lot about what your business is going to do and your Business Plan about how you are going to do it. Your Business Proposition will form an important part of your Business Plan and will fit into it when you write it. So work out your Business Proposition first.

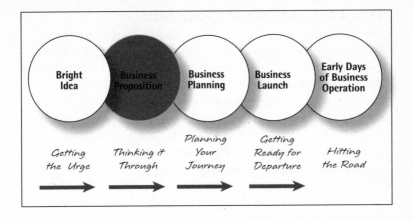

Bright
Idea

Business
Proposition

Business
Planning

Business
Launch

Early Days
of Business
Operation

Getting
the Urge

Thinking it
Through

Planning
Your
Journey

Getting
Ready for
Departure

Hitting
the Road

Customer First

Just because you think that your business has something great to offer doesn't mean that this is necessarily the case. Proof of this will only come when your customers start to buy from you. So start off by thinking about whatever you are proposing to launch from the perspective of your proposed customers. In return for your product or service you will be asking customers to part with their cash – sometimes their own hard-earned money and sometimes that of the company that they represent. You must describe a compelling offer to them that will motivate them to exchange their money for your product or service.

So what makes a proposition compelling from a customer's standpoint? Above all else, what you are offering should be grounded in at least one *customer need*. For example, 'I need to get across Birmingham quickly', or 'I need to remove a large amount of household waste material', or 'I need to have passport photographs taken', or 'I need a piece of jewellery to wear at a wedding'. You should think hard about what these needs really are and make sure that your product or service will satisfy them. Without the ability to do this you will not be able to persuade anyone to exchange their cash, at least of their own free will or for very long, for your products and services. Your proposition should be described in language that your customers, and anyone else who will be required to communicate with your customers (such as your staff or the media), will be able to clearly understand.

The 8-Point Business Proposition

The 8-Point Business Proposition allows you to methodically think through your business idea and then capture your thinking in one place. Some of the eight points need just a few words, some need expanding quite a bit. Once you've thought these through you will have a large part of what you need to really get your business moving from concept into reality, so take some time on this – it's the centrepiece or hub of everything from now on and will feed into almost everything that you will do if you get your business going. The 8-Point Business Proposition is:

1 **Business Name** – What is your business called?

2 **Business Description** – What does your business do?

3 **Market Opportunity** – Which market, sector or industry are you in?

4 **Target Markets** – Which customers are you specifically aiming at?

5 **Customer Needs** – What needs are you going to meet?

6 **Customer Offer** – What are you selling to meet these needs?

7 **Selling Points** – Why should the customer buy from you?

8 **Competition and Differentiation** – How will you be different to your competitors?

It's likely that you will have already got some of this content in your mind. It's unlikely, if you are being honest with yourself, that you have it all covered. But by going thoroughly through the Business Proposition development process you will fill the gaps and improve the chances of it working well in the market. We have provided some tools and templates for you to use to help you structure and capture your thinking. If you cannot clearly answer all of these points, you should seriously consider whether or not you are doing the right thing in starting this business – your chances of success will be limited.

Your 8-Point Business Proposition Described

1. Business name

You will no doubt have a name for your business in mind. Many people get overly concerned about their business name. Others get the name almost before they think of anything else. While finding the right name for your business is important, it's not that important. Don't spend hours twisting yourself in knots trying to think of something original, clever, cryptic or witty. It may be number one in our list here but really it ranks low in our order of priority.

Whatever you do decide to name your baby, pick something that you feel comfortable with. It's usually a good idea when you are starting off to choose a name that is recognisable to your customers and describes what the business does. For example, Styx Jewellery or Clintons Cards or ABC Taxis. This can be helpful if not essential in the early stages of your development because it means that customers instantly recognise what you do; it has a better chance of being picked up in search engines, and you do not need to think about spending money on trying to build a brand.

You're going to have to live with this name for quite a while – it will be on your business card, at the top of your letterhead, on your website, email signature, in sales material and mentioned in press, advertising and the media (if you're lucky!). You are going to say it out loud in front of other people, so make sure it's not embarrassing and can be clearly heard and understood. It should also be able to stand the test of time, so be careful of choosing something too topical or trendy. In the middle of the dotcom boom in the late 1990s we were going to call a business 'e-launchpartner.com'. This may have sounded good at the time but would sound very old-fashioned now.

Whatever name you choose, check that the name you have chosen does not conflict with existing companies, particularly in your market or industry. If not, you could find other organisations taking legal action – it will imply that you are trying to use their name and reputation for your benefit and this is not acceptable. Also, make sure that you can obtain a web address from a domain name supplier (technically known as a domain name registrar) that is the same or very similar to your chosen business name. There are thousands of domain name registrars in the UK alone and it's very simple to go to one of their sites, enter your proposed name and see if it's still available. Go to www.nominet.org.uk, which is the home of the '.uk' names for a comprehensive list of domain name registrars or simply use a search engine to find them.

By way of example, we are going to use a fictional small business in its early stages to illustrate how to put together your Business Proposition as we go through the eight points. In this case the fictitious business is called:

Styx Jewellery
www.styxjewellery.co.uk

2. Business description

You need to be able to describe what your business does in terms that can easily be understood. It should be concise so it might take you a while to get a succinct distillation of what you are doing. Have a go at trying to do this as you sit there now – if you thought that this was easy you may have just found out that it is not. It's often useful to try this out at an early stage on a friend, possibly your most critical or honest friend. To start with it can be a real challenge to find the right words to describe what your business does. This is quite normal at this stage. Keep trying and don't give up until you've written this down.

In our workshops at Bright Ideas Trust we ask participants to describe what their businesses do. Here's one attempt that shows what not to do. Michael said, 'We supply high quality niche products to the urban style market.' Try putting this description in the 'What We Do' section of your website or in a brochure and see if you attract any customers. It's unclear and riddled with jargon that no one will want to bother trying to understand. How about: 'Our business specifies, buys and imports good quality but low cost very fashionable clothes for the 14–25 female market from overseas manufacturers and then sells these through a number of small independent boutiques in London and the South East.' It's the same business, although it took us quite a while to work with Michael to find the right words to use.

Try to make your business description sound interesting and appealing to people and give them a chance to understand it. It's been said that you should try to make it so that your mum could understand it – that may be a stretch in some cases, but it does give you the general idea of what you should be trying to achieve. If you are going to be looking for funding for your business you will need to be able to clearly describe what your business does so that the potential investor can calibrate what you do against other possible destinations for their investment. Don't imagine that you can find a way around this point – they will want to know and if you cannot tell them they will usually become frustrated if they cannot understand (and switch off their attention) and go to find something more interesting to do with their time. They will also worry that if you can't explain it to them, how will you get on with your customers?

Sometimes it can be useful to come up with a short, succinct 'strapline' that you can put alongside your business name to convey to people very quickly what you will do for them.

For Styx Jewellery the business description is:

> **Styx Jewellery designs, makes and sells a range of jewellery products. Our products are necklaces, earrings, bracelets, rings and broaches. We sell these through our own website at www.styxjewellery.co.uk.**

The strapline is 'Brilliant bling at wicked prices'

3. Market opportunity

Work out which market you are in and get a good feel for it's size. When deciding on which markets you will be aiming your business at, first make sure that there is one. Are you sure? It's good to try to find a large and well-established market because it provides proof that there are customers with needs who are willing to part with their cash to buy existing products and services. So you will be faced with the challenge of getting these customers to buy your product or service over someone else's, rather than the greater challenge of competing in a small market with limited opportunities, or of creating an entirely new market. And although operating in a large and well-established market will mean that there will be many other suppliers competing for the customers, there will also be a lot more opportunity than if you pick a sector that is smaller or newly developing. Remember, you will need to generate a sufficient quantity of sales to make your business sustainable, so try to work in a market where there is enough demand from customers to allow you to do this. There are a few things to look out for.

Be realistic about what 'your' market is – if you are starting a building business your market will probably not be the total UK market for building services, at least not to begin with. More realistically, you will be operating in the building services market in your local area. This may be more difficult to establish, so take a proportion of the total market that might cover, say a fifty-mile radius of where you are based.

You don't need to know the market size down to the last pound note, just an approximation. You can usually find the overall market size by doing some basic research – with a bit of Internet searching or a trip to your local library you will be able to find this. For Styx Jewellery:

> **Styx operates in the jewellery products market. Sales via our website can be made to consumers anywhere in the world (the global market is estimated to be worth £100bn per year) but we market our goods in the UK and this is our primary market (estimated to be worth £1.5bn per year).**

4. Target markets

Who are your specific target customers? It's unlikely that you will be able to go after every single customer in the market. As we have seen above, even though you may believe that you can sell to anyone in the world, in reality you will be operating in a small section of the total market. And focusing on just some parts of the total market is a sensible thing to do anyway. You need to select a smaller subset of the overall market and focus on that, so that you have something manageable and controllable to aim at.

Most markets, particularly large markets, can be sub-divided into a number of smaller 'market segments' and indeed almost all businesses do some form of sub-segmentation even if they don't always consciously realise that they are doing it. Each market segment is different from other segments in the overall market and within each segment the customers will tend to have similar needs and wants and can be marketed and sold to by you in the same way. For example, for a photography business you might decide to focus on women who are planning weddings, schools requiring student portraits and newspaper editors looking for pictures for their publications. Clearly there are a myriad of potential markets for a photographer but it would be difficult to cover them all. So select your key target markets and beware of doing more than that at least until you are well established.

> **Styx Jewellery has chosen to focus on two target markets:**
> - **Consumers – Men aged 16–24**
>   - **Market Size (UK only) = 2.3m**
>   - **Market Value (UK only) = £600m p.a.**
>
> - **Consumers – Women aged 16–24**
>   - **Market Size (UK only) = 2.4m**
>   - **Market Value (UK only) = £900m p.a.**

To some extent your product or service will direct you to the proposed target market – for example, if you're selling women's jewellery you have already eliminated most men (although some could buy as presents for women and you might want to target them as a specific group). You can further refine your target market selection based on income bracket or where they shop or ethnic/ cultural background and so on.

So your Business Proposition needs to clearly state two or three market segments that you are going to aim at; how you are defining these segments, and why you are targeting them.

5. Customer needs

Now that you think you know which customers you're targeting, think specifically about what customer needs you are going to satisfy with what you have to offer. Customer needs are to your business what the location of a property is to an estate agent. So where they say that the three most important things in determining the appeal of a property are 'Location Location, Location', you should be thinking that the three most important things in determining your proposition are 'Needs, Needs, Needs'. These needs are sometimes referred to as Points of Pain. Think of your potential customers as being in mild discomfort – they are crying out for something to ease their pain. It doesn't matter what the pain is, but what can you offer to help them become satisfied? What can I do to help me to understand the needs of potential customers?

You can try doing a bit of market research for yourself. Research need not be as dry and boring as it might sound – it can be an interesting and valuable thing to do to help you launch a good business. Research does not need to involve spending hours in the local library or interviewing strangers in your local high street, although doing these things can help. The purpose of research is principally to help you feel more secure about what you are proposing to do with your business, practical things which you can see are relevant, not just gathering market statistics for the sake of it or to satisfy someone else, like an investor.

Practical research can often be equally if not more valuable than statistics and analysis – often what you see and feel are just as important as what you think. Look around, see what your potential competitors are doing; don't be frightened to ask your potential customers how they feel about what you might offer and what they can buy at the moment. And use your judgement, your nose for what's right, rather than relying on pure statistics.

Try standing in the shoes of the customer – look at what you are proposing to offer from the customer's perspective. One effective way of doing this once you have decided which customers you are going to target with your product or services is to try to become one of them for a few minutes. Put yourself in their position as someone who is being approached by your company and think about what needs you might be trying to satisfy and what solutions might be able to achieve this. You are never going to be able to do this completely – every customer is slightly different – but try and it should help you. This exercise is about developing *empathy* with your customers, trying to get inside their minds to understand what makes them buy and what you need to do to make them buy your products and services.

When the Japanese were starting to dominate the car manufacturing market in the 1980s they sent their designers to live with American families so that they could be with them every day to see how they were using their cars and what they really needed. They went shopping with them, did the school run with them, and went on family visits with them. These people literally stood in the shoes of the customer. With the knowledge gained from living the life of their customer they were better able to create cars that were exactly what these customers wanted and as a result beat their (typically American) competition.

However, bear in mind that the customer is not always right – you need to listen to customers and then use your judgement about whether what they are telling you is really right. There is a balance to be achieved between what customers tell you that they want and what you think is right for them and your business to be successful. Always err on the side of the customer and do not be so arrogant as to think that you are always right – this is a certain way to failure. But remember Henry Ford's words when he said, 'If I'd asked the customers what they wanted I would have given them faster horses.' So make sure that you are sure that what you are offering can truly meet the needs of your target customers.

> **Styx Jewellery meets the following customer needs:**
> - **Men aged 21–30: Need to make a fashion statement through wearing jewellery, so**

important that item is seen as unique and not worn by everyone. Strong peer group pressure to own and display these items. Want to make investment in tangible and valuable items that could be sold again later if needed.

- Women aged 21–30: Need a piece of jewellery to wear every day, but must be different from the crowd and not worn by any other woman in peer group. Needs to be precious metal and seen as genuine article so cannot be seen as cheap. Want to make investment in tangible and valuable item that could be sold again later if needed.

6. Customer offer

What are you offering to meet your chosen customers' needs? The 'Customer Offer' is another way of describing the product and/or service that you are providing. Will your business sell products or services or a mixture of both? For example, if you have a hairdressing business you will doubtless be washing, cutting, colouring and drying (these are services) but you may also sell hair gel, shampoo, conditioner (these are products).

Each offer should match the needs of each of your target markets with a clear description of what you are offering to that group that will satisfy those needs in a compelling (the customer should be driven by the power of your offer to buy from you) and sustainable (the customer will come back to buy more from you) way. Your Customer Offer should try to answer the following questions – and from the customers' perspective:

- What is it – is it a product or a service or a bit of both and what does it do?

- **Why do I need it – will it meet one or more needs that I have?**
- **What benefits will it give me – if I use it what will it do for me?**
- **How does it compare to alternatives available – why should I buy yours rather than someone else's?**
- **Where can I buy it – in a shop, online, through mail order, over the phone?**
- **What will it cost me – the price, including any post-purchase payments such as maintenance or support?**

Don't try to come up with too many different offers to your customers. The most important thing to do is to focus on doing a small number of things really well. You will usually have very limited resources (money, people, time) in a start-up so use them wisely and in a targeted way to give your customers something really excellent. Keep things simple, at least to start with; you can expand your range when you are more established.

By doing these things, the trick is to try to avoid simply competing on having a lower price – it's easy to give stuff away or sell it cheaper than anyone else, but you will find it harder and harder to make money if you start from this position. Concentrate on getting some sort of competitive edge in your chosen market so that customers will buy from you rather than from someone else. By providing greater value than someone else, you can even charge more for it. So think hard about how your product or service is going to be differentiated from other things in the market place.

How do I price my offer? There are many ways to do this and you can find some extraordinarily complicated formulae and calculations out there if you take a look. Once again, keep it simple and remember that pricing is more of an art than a science. The immediate inclination of many is to simply go for a Cost Plus approach – what did it cost you to make or buy in the product or service that you are selling? Then add on an amount that you need to make to cover all your costs and make a profit. Whilst this is simple and may appear attractive to you it is not recommended because it takes no account of what is happening in the market or what the customer is willing to pay. A better starting point is to do Market Pricing – what do customers currently expect to pay in the market? Then make sure that your price is somewhere in that ballpark. It's very difficult to start charging amounts over what the competition is charging unless you really have something spectacular to beat it. On the other hand, you do not want to price too low, even if you think that this will get you lots of sales, because it can lead to the impression that there must be a catch and put customers off. And, of course, you may not be able to make a profit if you do this. So there's always a delicate balance to be achieved when doing your pricing.

When you first introduce your product or service you might consider offering it at a lower price to 'penetrate' the market. This is always tempting because it can give you a way to get quick sales. Going cheaper than everyone else in the market is easy, but it's often unsustainable over a long period unless you can achieve very high volumes of sales. Try offering short-term discounts (10 per cent off introductory offer) or package deals (2 for the price of 1) for a short period and then getting your price back to a sustainable level later. It's easy to drop your price but can be much harder to raise it so start off as high as you think the market will bear and offer short-term price reductions or special time-limited offers.

Returning again to our jewellery business, it might articulate the customer offer as follows:

> **Styx Jewellery makes and sells a range of highly fashionable/ limited edition jewellery products – Necklaces, Bracelets, Earrings, Rings and Broaches. All our products are made of silver or gold or a mix of both and each piece is inlaid with our signature cubic zirconia stones. There is nothing quite like it on the market. Our products are right for you if you want to**

wear something at a special occasion, as a present for someone, or as a thank you. By wearing a piece of our jewellery you have the opportunity to publicly demonstrate that you are different from the crowd – each piece is hand crafted and there are only a few of each type made. While there are a few other suppliers of this type of jewellery, they charge four to five times as much for a similar product to ours. Also, we specifically make our pieces so that they are attractive to younger people rather than for older and perceived wealthier markets as is the case with other makers. You can buy our products at www.styxjewellery.co.uk or at Little Norton market on Saturdays and Thursdays. Prices range from £40 to £400 to the end consumer.

7. Selling points

We've all heard of the phrase Unique Selling Point or USP. It's a much overused and abused term. Originally, the U in USP really meant Unique but nowadays it's used much more loosely to cover any sort of differentiating point that you might have over your competition.

So don't even think about the need to be unique – there is not much in the world these days that has not already been done that is truly unique, so don't lose any sleep in trying to think of something completely new – you will never get your business started. Just be able to do something better, faster, cheaper, friendlier, something that customers will want to buy ahead of someone else.

Turn what you believe to be your advantages over your competitors into a strong set of selling points compared to what they have to offer. If you do not have any you will probably struggle to make your product seem attractive to customers. Selling points can include how your version of a product or service is better than others, what extra or different features/functions it has, more attractive pricing, better delivery arrangements/time, improved customer service, better after sales support, and so on. Or they could be all about you – personal qualities you or people working for you have that can give you an edge over the competition. For example, local camera shops still do well against the big suppliers on the Internet because they can offer specialist advice and support – and this is what certain customers need.

So be clear about what your selling points are and be ready to use them – you never know when this might be, so be prepared. For Styx Jewellery the selling point might be:

- **Stunning contemporary designs by a leading UK jewellery designer**
- **Solid, durable and stylish manufacture**
- **Hand made in our small workshop by skilled craftspeople, not mass produced**
- **Prices lower than comparable products in the market so good value for money**
- **Choose from a range of designs online for delivery within 48 hours via our website**
- **Great customer service – we respond to your queries by email or phone within four hours during working day**

8. Competition and differentiation

Which brings us on to the final piece of the pie. What do you do better than your competition and how will you beat it? How will you be different in the eyes of your customer from what is already available to them?

When we interview people looking for support for their new venture we frequently hear them say that they have no competition. Yeah, right! So do try not to embarrass yourself by ever saying this or convince yourself that this might be true. You always have competition. And it's a good thing. It proves that there is a market with customers and needs out there because someone is already supplying it. Even if the situation ever existed where you really were the 'only game in town' (and we can't think of many monopolies these days), you will still be competing with the most dangerous competitor of all. This competitor is called 'Do Nothing', because the customer can choose to buy nothing at all, just sit on their hands, keep their cash in their pocket and do without. In many ways this is the worst competitor of all: you cannot see it and it gives you no reasons as to why it has beaten you.

Make a list of all the businesses that you can think of that are providing some or all of the things that you are proposing to offer to your customers. Be specific about this – you are not competing with everyone in the world. If you are setting up a high-street retail outlet then you are competing with other retail outlets that sell similar products to you within a limited geographical area, say, a five-mile radius. But you may also be competing with out-of-town shops, and well-known online retailers – if you're a bookseller then clearly amazon and many others will probably be your competitors.

There's an old saying that you should 'keep you friends close but keep your enemies closer'. So start taking a keen interest and a regular look at what all of your competitors are offering and keep on doing this throughout the life of your business.

Try listing all the ways (maybe it's just one way) that you are genuinely different from what your competitors are offering. It might be a function of your product (IKEA furniture is simple to assemble) or your service (Google originally made its name by returning your search enquiry faster than other search engines).

Styx competes with three main types of competitors:

- **High-street jewellers – sell mainly mass-produced, commodity-type products**
- **'Bond Street' jewellers – sell high-end jewellery similar to Styx**
- **Online jewellery retailers – they sell a wide range of products, including some similar to Styx**

Summary of Styx Jewellery Business Proposition

1. Business Name	5. Customer Needs
Styx Jewellery www.styxjewellery.co.uk	Styx Jewellery meets the following customers needs: • Men aged 21–30: Need to make a fashion statement through wearing jewellery so important that item is seen as unique and not worn by everyone. Strong peer group pressure to own and display these items. Want to make investment in tangible and valuable item that could be sold again later if needed.
2. Business Description	
Styx Jewellery designs, makes and sells a range of jewellery products. Our products are necklaces, earrings, bracelets and rings and broaches we sell these through our own website at (www.styxjewellery.co.uk).	• Women aged 21–30: Need a piece of jewellery to wear every day, but must be different from the crowd and not worn by any other woman in peer group. Needs to be precious metal and seen as genuine article so cannot be seen as cheap. Want to make investment in tangible and valuable item that could be sold again later if needed.
3. Market Opportunity	
Styx operates in the jewellery products market. Sales via our website can be made to consumers anywhere in the world (the global market is estimated to be worth £100bn per year) but we market our goods in the UK and this is our primary market (estimated to be worth £1.5bn per year).	**6. Customer Offer**
	Styx Jewellery makes and sells a range of highly fashionable/limited edition jewellery products – Necklaces, Bracelets, Earrings, Ring and Broaches. All our products are made of silver or gold or a mix of both and each piece is inlayed with our signature cubic zirconia stones. There is nothing quite like it on the market. Our products are right for you if you want to wear something special at a special occasion, as a present for someone else or as a thank you. By wearing a piece of our jewellery you have the opportunity to publicly demonstrate that you are different from the crowd – each piece is hand-made and there are only a few of each type
4. Target Markets	
Styx Jewellery focuses on 2 target markets:	
Consumers – Men aged 16–24 Market Size (UK only) = 2.3m people Market Value (UK only) = £600m p.a.	
Consumers – Women aged 16–24 Market Size (UK only) = 2.4m people Market Value (UK only) = £900m p.a.	

	made. Whilst there are a few other suppliers of this type of jewellery, they charge four to five times as much for a similar product to ours. Also, we specifically make our pieces so that they are attractive to younger people rather than for older and perceived wealthier market as is the case with other makers. You can buy our products at www.styxjewellery.co.uk or at Little Norton market on Saturdays and Thursdays. Prices range from £40 to £400 to the end consumer.
	7. Selling Points
	• Stunning contemporary designs by a leading UK jewellery designer • Solid, durable and stylish manufacture • Hand made in our small workshop by skilled craftspeople, not mass produced • Prices lower than comparable products in the market so good value for money • Choose from a range of designs on line for delivery within 48 hours via our website • Great customer service – we respond to your queries by email or phone within 4 hours during working day.
	8. Competition & Differentiation
	Styx competes with three main types of competitors: • High street jewelers – selling mainly mass produced, commodity type products • 'Bond Street' Jewelers – sell high-end jewellery similar to Styx On line jewellery retailers – they sell a wide range of products, including some similar to Styx.

The One-Page Business Proposition Summary

This brings all the points of your proposition into one single place to allow you to see if it all fits together as a single coherent picture of what you are proposing to offer to your customer. Once you have it, try to look at it from your customers' viewpoint – how would they react to what it says about what you are proposing to offer? Would they say that what you have in mind is attractive and different or might they just say it's all right but they could get something similar from many other places already? Then try it out on a few people that you know and see what feedback they give you. It might be perfect! Or more likely you might find that you need to tweak it in one way or another, or you might need to go back to square one. Either way, this is a tried and tested approach to bringing your business idea to life and seeing if it might work before you start spending money and investing your time in launching it.

Opposite is the completed one-page Business Proposition for Styx Jewellery.

Business Proposition – What's the Point?

Strong foundations – The Business Proposition is at the core of everything that you will do with your business going forward. It is the foundation of your venture. Create bad foundations and you will at worst fail further down the road and at best be starting over in order to survive later.

Make once, use many – The material that you produce when you write down your Business Proposition will be reusable in many ways as you go forward. For example:

- In sales presentation material
- In pitches to potential investors and funders
- To write PR or press material
- In brochures and for your website

- *To brief suppliers and attract partners*
- *To recruit staff*

Once you have it you have a strong platform from which to launch everything else that you do. It will give you a framework within which you will think about getting on to the next stages of starting your business.

U-turn if you want to – Your Business Proposition will undoubtedly change as you go through the process, sometimes more than you might imagine as your thinking develops. Don't be worried about that, just capture your thoughts as you go along and refine them as and when appropriate. As the owner of your own business you have the prerogative to change your mind on what your proposition is at any time once you've launched, such as when a new customer need suddenly appears or if you find that what you thought of as being irresistible to customers is failing. This is one of the great advantages over working for someone else – you can change what you're doing without asking for the grown-ups' permission.

Why spend time on it?

- *SANITY CHECK – So that you don't make any obvious mistakes. We've worked on the development of a large number of business propositions over the years. In that time we've worked with people with dreams of creating a Fortune 500 or FTSE 100 company out of their great new idea. All they needed was a bit of funding, to get out there and the world would be theirs. Without wishing to dampen anyone's enthusiasm at this point, we have to say that many of the propositions we've worked on have never got past the first few days of trying to make them clear, and others where we got all the way through the process and then saw that the business as designed would not have worked. This is no bad thing – it can save everyone a lot of time* and money by stopping at this stage — so use this as a thorough check on what you're proposing

- **DON'T FOOL YOURSELF** — It forces you to be honest with yourself about whether or not you can turn your idea into a sustainable and viable business. You can try to fool your parents or a teacher or the law or a friend (we've all done it) but right now you've only got yourself to fool, so don't bother trying. Take self-responsibility. At this stage you are allowed to say, 'I don't know': in fact it's better if you do. Indeed if you don't say, 'I don't know', then there is probably something very wrong with what you are doing. Also remember that you may be asking others to put their money into your business to support you and you will not want to let them down

- **IMPROVE** — So that you work out how to really make your business the best it can be. A little bit of extra thinking can make a huge difference to what you do. Once you have the basic proposition worked out, then you can often see opportunities to enrich it

- **LOUD & CLEAR** — You need to write down in clear language what your Business Proposition is. It needs to be clear to someone who knows nothing much about what you are planning so that they can understand it. Why does it need to be clear? Because the chances are that someone will be one of your customers and if the customer cannot understand it they probably won't buy from you, and then you will have wasted your time. You will want to get feedback on your ideas and the emerging proposition as it develops — look for lots of it at all stages along this journey

More Haste, Less Speed

Don't expect to have this all worked out on day one. It should take you a while to thoroughly think through your proposition – when you look at the Styx Jewellery example you may already be able to see ways that it could be improved, or flaws in its proposition – there should always be room for improvement. When we were developing the Business Proposition for CESQ, a business that was planning to provide a range of male grooming products, we took about eight weeks, spending ten to fifteen hours per week, to think it all through properly. We met twice a week on average for a few hours per session, 'white boarded' our thoughts and then took those away and wrote them up. We shared that by email and then started the next session with a review of what we'd got so far and looked at where we had gaps in our thinking that we needed to plug. This process was repeated until we had a well-thought-through document that covered all the main points of the proposed Business Proposition. Then we tested it on a few people, took their feedback, and revised again.

It's not a race but equally it shouldn't be done too slowly either. Don't take for ever trying to get everything perfect. You should set yourself a time limit, a deadline, and force yourself to have done enough thinking through by that time – get it done in six to ten weeks, no more, no less. If it takes longer than that it's probably because the idea is not going anywhere (and you don't want to admit it – which is one of the biggest barriers to getting all new businesses off the ground) or because you're losing focus or interest. Forcing yourself to make time to do this, being disciplined about sitting down on a regular and planned basis and not making it easy for yourself is an important part of what's required to be successful in business.

PLANNING YOUR JOURNEY

BUSINESS PLAN

'By failing to prepare, you are preparing to fail.' Benjamin Franklin

Whenever people talk about business the words 'business plan' always come up. You have taken the time in the previous chapter to work out what your Business Proposition is, so now we can look at why and when you will need to put together a Business Plan. This section also provides a simple framework within which to put together a short and concise Business Plan and offers practical advice and guidance on how to make the most of your plan.

What's a Business Plan?

You have chosen and got enthusiastic about your business idea, thought through how this might succeed in the market place using some tried and tested tools described above and maybe even found yourself a mentor and discussed it all with them. You are now ready to write your Business Plan.

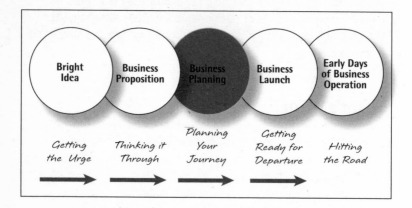

The idea of writing a Business Plan can sometimes strike dismay into the heart of any would-be business owner. It's a bit like doing the revision for an exam – you can always find something else to do while you put it off. But the day will almost certainly come when you have to face up to it. But with very few exceptions every successful business has at some stage written some form of Business Plan.

Writing it down is an important stage in the journey, although many find it difficult or at least uncomfortable to do this, especially when all you want to do is get on and sell your products or services. There are several reasons for this reluctance. Some, including a good number of really successful business people, are not that great at writing. Some may believe that they can get away without doing it. Some, if they are honest, may not have that much content to include in a plan and take the approach that, as Mark Twain said, 'It is better to keep your mouth closed and let people think you are a fool than to open it and remove all doubt.' Some businesses have been launched from the virtually incomprehensible scribblings on a napkin after a late night or the seemingly mad ramblings of an inspirational leader, but don't bank on this happening to you. We mere mortals will usually need to have a document that summarises what we are trying to do so that we are very clear in our minds, have thought through the important issues, have not missed anything and can communicate our aims with others.

In the same way that you need to clearly articulate your overall Business Proposition and what you are offering your potential customers, you will need to write down a Business Plan. This is where you will turn all your thinking into a written document that will become a roadmap for what your business will do and how it will do it.

What's it For?

Most people's immediate thought is that they only need to write a Business Plan if they are looking to raise funding for their business. Although this is one of the major reasons why a Business Plan should be written, you should do one even if this is not your aim. Your Business Plan will get your thoughts out of your head and on to paper to give you a continual reminder of what you hope your business will become. And it will be your roadmap to refer to. Here are a few of the reasons for putting your plan together:

- *REALITY CHECK* – *Your plan provides you with a reality check on what you are planning and should give you no hiding place from any deficiencies or holes in your approach. Writing a plan forces you once again to think it all through properly – and sometimes to admit if you don't know things, encouraging you to go away and find the solution to make the plan work*

- *SALES PITCH* – *Think of your Business Plan as one of the first pieces of sales material that you will produce. Your first customer of this might be someone that you are trying to persuade to provide funding to get your business started. If you are trying to persuade someone to fund your business it will be vital that it sells to them what you are* proposing to do, describing how exciting this business is going to be as well as showing how you are going to make it a success. Crucially, it needs to give a picture of how you and any external funders will achieve a return on investment in your business

- **OPERATIONAL PLANNING TOOL** – Your plan is a guide to you as to what you need to do to launch and run your business. While it's not intended as a step-by-step manual to be slavishly followed, it should give you a good direction at least to start with. Once you get going the plan is also a way of checking back to see that you are on target and ensuring that you do what you said you were going to do at the outset. If you have one, investors will expect you to show them progress against the original plan that they backed

- **CRYSTAL BALL** – Think of your Business Plan as a forecast based on your best judgement of what is going to happen in the future with your business. You're saying to yourself, and others who will read it, 'This is what I think is going to happen with my business and this is how I am going to make that happen.'

- **COMMUNICATION TOOL** – Your Business Plan is a way of sharing what you intend to do with other people, particularly when you first start to put it together. It is important to get their feedback so that you can spot any gaps, take on board other people's ideas and improve it

- **FUNDRAISING TOOL** – As we said, you will have no option but to do a formal Business Plan if you're looking to raise financing. So think of it as an application form or a sales brochure to potential investors or supporters for funding for your business. If you don't fill out the application, you

cannot get the funds. And remember to make it a
good application because the person you are
sending it to has probably got a number of other
applications sitting on their desk competing for
their attention and limited cash

What Do I Do?

There is no fixed definition of what should be in your Business Plan. You can find instruction on, templates for, and examples of a multitude of ways to prepare a plan – there are books, guides, leaflets and nowadays megabytes worth of information on the Internet. Just Google 'Business Plans' and you'll see what we mean. We do not, therefore, propose to provide you with a step-by-step guide to how to write your Business Plan and cannot assert that you should only do it our way.

However, through a combination of seeing what tends to work best in the venture capital world, preparing plans for fundraising for our own businesses and working with young people to prepare Business Plans over the last few years at Bright Ideas Trust, we aim to give you a good idea of what's needed in the real world.

Whatever you do, it's important to treat it as a statement of fact, not a work of fiction. While it needs to be optimistic and attractive to potential investors, it must be truthful. You will want to put the best spin on your plans but if you feel the desire to be 'economical with the truth' this will almost always come out later because a funder or investor will want to know all about your business, usually through the Due Diligence process which will always reveal what you may be trying to conceal.

How Long Does it Need to Be?

A Business Plan can be anything from just a few pages long to a lengthy and detailed document. If you are the only audience for it – in other words you are not going to use it to help you to raise money – you can usually produce a good summary in a few pages. If you are looking for funding, the length and amount of detail in the plan will almost certainly be more and will depend upon three main factors:

- *AMBITION* – *The scale and scope of your business. For example, if you're a sole trader setting up a painting and decorating business you will need to give less detail than a group of partners setting up a new mobile phone service provider business*

- *AMOUNT* – *How much you are seeking to raise – typically the greater the sum required, the more detail required*

- *SOURCE* – *Where you are looking to get this from – if you were seeking major funding from a venture capital company you would need to produce a document of possibly forty to fifty pages (or more) containing considerable detail of a wide range of aspects of your proposed business. By contrast, if you were applying to Bright Ideas Trust or some other business support organisations for a few hundred or thousand pounds, you might only need to produce a few pages. If you're looking for a bank loan then you will probably need a business plan somewhere between these two, although a good ten-to-twenty-pager will probably get you a long way here*

Note that this list does not include the complexity of your bright idea – even the most sophisticated idea can be reduced to a concise summary if you work at it long enough!

We've reviewed thousands of Business Plans over the years and the best ones are always short, concise and succinct. The worst ones usually resemble *War and Peace*, although without the content. They tend to be long-winded, repetitive and well padded with waffle – often with parts cut and pasted from other documents, including straight from the Internet. Remember, if you're trying to raise funding your plan is a sales document intended to get you to a first meeting with someone at which you will have the chance to fully explain in great detail all about your business. So use it to get you through the door only – just enough, not too much. Like your CV when you're looking for a job – it won't get you the job, that's for the interview, but it will get you an interview.

So if you're looking for external funding or investment think in terms of a plan that will be anything from twenty to fifty pages long. Make sure that you have a punchy two-to-three-page summary at the beginning.

If you're doing the plan just for yourself, think in terms of ten to twenty pages. Again, it's worth doing the brief summary as well.

In reality, when you write a Business Plan it's actually much harder to write less, and get all the information required into it, than more. But this is what you should be aiming to do, so expect it to take you longer to write less! So ask yourself, 'Can I get all my thoughts about what my business is going to be about into ten or twenty well-written pages?' Overall, we would recommend that you stick to the old adage that 'small is beautiful'.

Business Plan Structure

Broadly speaking think of your Business Plan as being made up of two main parts. These are:

- *WORDS – Description of what your business is all about set out in a few sub-sections; and*

- *NUMBERS – The financial forecasts for the business and how you will turn your words (above) into profit and create a sustainable business*

This chapter deals with the Words, the next chapter goes into how you do the Numbers.

Words

Try this . . . imagine yourself on the other side of the desk to the person who's just received your plan that includes a request for funds. Put yourself in their shoes for a moment. Your pride and joy has landed on their desk along with all the others they've got that day. Think of them as an impatient, irritable stranger who has heard all of this before – if you can convince them of what you are proposing then this should show that you are on the right lines.

First of all, your plan needs to look something like the sort of document they're expecting – they will have a mental picture of what it should look like for a business that they might like to get involved with. They're used to seeing it done a certain way. They don't want to see something much different to that because they're thinking in terms of comparing yours to what they're used to seeing. It's their frame of reference. They've probably got a lot of these to look through and they want to make life as easy as possible for themselves. When working with a leading venture capital firm Paul looked at about 2,000 plans in one year. That's about ten for every working day in that year, that's about one an hour, every hour of his working life.

So you need to give them what they want. Your plan needs to be concise, have all the required elements, have a very good summary – the reader will not go further if this is no good – and have an 'ask' from the recipient – what do you want from them? They will almost always read the Executive Summary at least so it's vital that this gets straight to the point and clearly lays out what your business is all about.

As we said, you will see all sorts of different ways and read much jargon about the contents of Business Plans. But when you break them down, all Business Plans essentially have four main parts:

1   Executive Summary

2   Description of Your Business Proposition

3   How you will Implement Your Business Proposition

4   Financial Matters and Keeping Control

1. Executive Summary

This is a brief, punchy and succinct overall summary of the key points contained in the rest of your Business Plan. It's usually called an Executive Summary although it could equally be called the 'I haven't got the time to spend on this, just give me the facts so that I can get on with other things' summary, or the 'I'm easily bored and my eyes glaze over if I have to read more than two pages' summary, or 'This is what I get from everyone else, so it's what I expect from you' summary. Bear all of these points in mind when you are thinking about putting a plan together because while they all may be irritating, they are all true. Anyway, it's a fancy title for a summary (probably to make the person to whom it's addressed feel important) and it should aim to get across your main points, the ones that you really want the reader to notice, as quickly and clearly as you possibly can. It needs to grab the readers' attention from the start.

It's also fair to say that because so many Business Plans are full of padding (usually because the author has an inability to get to the point or is making up for lack of quality of thought with quantity of words), the reader has every right to ask for you to get it all summarised in a few words.

Although it's at the start of the plan it's usually best to write it last so that you've got everything else done and can summarise it here. It should include:

- *WHAT IS YOUR BUSINESS PROPOSITION?*

  - *A brief summary of the main points of your proposition*

- *HOW WILL YOU DELIVER YOUR PROPOSITION TO YOUR CUSTOMERS BY IMPLEMENTING THIS PLAN?*

  - *A brief summary of the main actions you will take to make your plan happen*

- *HOW DOES YOUR BUSINESS MAKE A PROFIT?*

  - *A summary table showing the profit and loss account for the first few years of the business*

- *WHAT ARE YOU ASKING THE READER TO GIVE TO YOUR BUSINESS?*

  - *If funding – how much, what for and when do you need it?*

- If other support — what?

- WHAT WILL THEY GET IF THEY GET INVOLVED IN YOUR BUSINESS?

  - What financial return will they make?

  - Will they get any other benefit from it?

- WHAT IS YOUR EXIT STRATEGY?

  - If this is your goal, explain how you will sell your business in the future

2. Business Proposition

The core of the Business Plan is a section that describes your Business Proposition. This section describes concisely what your business is about and includes who your customers will be, what you're offering them, what benefits it provides them with, how you match up with the competition and how you will make money. If you've already read through our Business Proposition section you will have a good idea of what this will include. If you have already written up your Business Proposition then you will be able to slot it straight into the Business Plan. Congratulations, you have one of the four sections done already. But just to summarise:

- BUSINESS DESCRIPTION — Describe what your business will do. Imagine you are describing it to someone who has no idea about your area of business. Include a picture or illustration to help to show people what your business does

- MARKET OPPORTUNITY & NEEDS — Describe the market opportunity that you can exploit and the needs that exist in the market that your proposition meets. Set out how any changes in the market — social, economic, legal, environmental or technological — will mean your product/service has a greater opportunity that didn't exist in the past

- *TARGET MARKETS & CUSTOMER OFFERS –* Explain what different market segments you will sell to, what different needs they have and what your customer offer in each segment will be

- *MARKET OVERVIEW & COMPETITION –* Describe the market or industry you will be in, the changes taking place, the main players, and your immediate competition

- *DIFFERENTIATION AND SELLING POINTS* – Describe why customers will come to you rather than to another business or even just not buy anything at all

3. Implementation

This section shows how you are going to turn your thought-through proposition into a practical business that is operating and trading day-to-day. It should include short descriptions of the following things:

- *SALES & MARKETING PLANS –* What will you do to make customers aware of and inform them about your products and services, i.e., how you will promote them? How will you sell to your customers – retail, online, mail, directly yourself, through others, a combination of these?

- *OPERATIONAL PLANS –* Describe what you need to have in place before the business can operate successfully – office, vehicle, equipment, IT systems and computers

- *MANAGEMENT TEAM –* Describe who will be leading this business (it can be just you). State what roles they will play and what skills and experience they bring to the role. If roles need to be filled, say what they are. Enclose CVs for you and for other key staff if appropriate as appendices at the back of the plan

- **SUPPLIER ARRANGEMENTS** – Explain the important supplier relationships you will need to establish and maintain in order to succeed. Give details of specific suppliers that you have arrangements in place with or are speaking with

- **IMPLEMENTATION PLAN** – Describe the important things that will need to happen for the business to be fully operational and succeeding. Include a timetable to show the order and timing of the main things that need to be done

- **MILESTONES & MOMENTUM** – Show the reader what milestones you have achieved so far – any sales made, product built, staff hired, orders received, etc., and what things you are doing to generate momentum over the next few months – attending a conference, meeting with customers, doing product testing, interviewing staff, etc.

- **MAIN RISKS** – Set out what are the big things that could impact your plans, and what could you do to deal with them. Include only important risks that are within your control – you cannot do much about a global recession but can respond to your competitors dropping their prices. Using Styx Jewellery as an example:

4. Money and financial control

Your plan will need to contain some important information about how you are going to manage the finances of your business. If you are asking people to invest money into what you are doing then you will be required to help them feel comfortable about handing over their cash to you. Even if you are not seeking funding from outside, consider why you should put your own money (and time) into this business rather than something else. So you need to show *yourself* that you know what you are going to do financially and how you intend to manage things. And to provide yourself with a financial plan against which you can measure your performance month by month once you get into operation.

Financial backers will be especially interested in this part of the plan. Your plan needs to set out that it's all under control and that their money is going to be well managed by you, that they will get a healthy return on their investment and that they will be able to sleep well at night – to give them what they often call a warm feeling.

This part of the plan needs to cover the following:

- *FINANCIAL FORECAST – In the following chapter we explain in detail how to put together your financial forecast. In your plan you will need to provide a summary profit and loss account shown in a table, as shown in the example below:*

Profit & Loss Forecast	Year 1	Year 2	Year 3
Sales	10,000	50,000	75,000
Cost of goods sold	5,000	22,000	30,000
Gross Profit	**5,000**	**28,000**	**45,000**
Operating Costs	6,000	12,000	15,000
Net Profit	**–1,000**	**14,000**	**30,000**
Net Profit %	–10%	28%	40%

- *ASSUMPTIONS – You will probably not know all the information that will be required to complete a financial forecast at this stage. You might have a very clear idea about how much your raw materials might cost or how much you intend to pay yourself. But some things will be predictions – like how many sales you will make or the price that you will be able to achieve. So you need to explain what are the important assumptions you have made in arriving at these forecasts, and why you have decided on these values. The forecast is as much about the thinking behind the numbers that you have used as it is about the numbers themselves. If you are looking for funding, investors will want to see this – not so that they can beat you up or laugh at you – but so that they can understand how you think that the business will work and so that they can make an informed decision about the risk that they're being asked to take by investing in you. It's also helpful for you because it will give you some target prices and costs to aim at as you build the business*

KEY RISKS AND MITIGATION

Risk Area	Impact on your Business	What we will do to overcome it
Too few hits on our website	Inadequate sales to make income target	Increase marketing by search engine optimisation, viral marketing and banner advertising
Raw materials prices increase	Reduces profit margins	Find new suppliers, increase prices
Too much demand for our products	Poor customer service and orders lost as delivery time too long for customers	Build up a stock, change customer expectations for delivery

You will probably notice that all of the actions required to deal with the impact of these risks requires increased spending, so be prepared to answer questions on what this would involve.

■ *FUNDING REQUIREMENT – What funding do you need and what is it needed for? Say how much finance and time/resources you personally have already committed or will commit to the business. These figures will become obvious to you when you put together your cashflow forecast – we will*

*describe how to do this in the next chapter. Show
these in a table, as below:*

FUNDING REQUIREMENT

Use of Funds	Amount Required
Equipment Costs	£2,500
Raw Material Costs	£1,500
Website Design and Build Costs	£800
Total	**£4,800**

■ *EXIT STRATEGY – And finally, if you are
planning to create an equity-driven business, i.e.,
one that you are planning to sell to another
organisation or place on a public stock market,
then you will need to give some details of your
proposed exit strategy. In other words, who are the
likely acquirers of your business at some stage in
the future, when do you think you will be able to
sell (usually investors will want to see this
happening within five years)? Provide an outline
idea of what you think your business will be worth
at that time*

In the following pages we have provided a worked example of a
Business Plan using the framework outlined above. While this is not
a full Business Plan it gives you an idea of the sort of content that
you should be looking to include in your plan.

Company Name		Contact	Thomas Eliot
Toxic Solutions Limited	**TOXIC**™		3, Railway Sidings East Cheam Surrey
Company Stage	Start-Up/ Pre-Revenue	**Sector**	Technology, Innovative Mobile Communications Software
Year Started	2008	**Location**	Midlands

1. Business description

Toxic is an innovative mobile communications software business which has developed the technology to transform the way in which the Internet is delivered to, and consumed by, mobile phone users.

It has spent the last 24 months developing its unique software platform, user interface and billing capability which enables selected parts of any content provider's digital content to be simply, quickly and cheaply accessed, displayed and refreshed by the consumer on their mobile phone. This eliminates the use of browsers, URLs and bandwidth-hungry page downloads.

This plan describes how Toxic will create a large and well-profiled customer base by giving consumers free access to its software, so that they can easily get to their preferred content, and by opening its platform to third-party software developers allowing them to develop and sell mobile micro applications (apps) in partnership with Toxic.

It will mainly generate revenues from digital advertisers, agencies and marketers who will be able to display highly targeted advertising via the Toxic system on the consumer's phone as well as from content providers and consumers who will buy a range of Toxic applications.

Figure 1

The Toxic software platform consists of a Framework and User Interface plus one or more micro-applications (apps) to deliver desired web content to the mobile user.

Figure 1 shows Toxic delivering comprehensive, real-time interaction with the user's My eBay account through an eBay APP.

Figure 2

The Toxic software platform also allows one or more unrelated or 'stand-alone' APP to deliver desired web content to the mobile user.

Figure 2 shows Toxic delivering a Stockwatch service through an app which may be personalised to show the desired stock and which automatically and regularly updates.

2. Market opportunity & business drivers

The market for digital mobile content is expanding very rapidly on a global scale driven by:

■ Mobile service providers seeking ways to replace falling voice revenues

■ Rapid consumer uptake of powerful 'Smartphones' (forecast by Leading Research Company Limited to be up from 100m in 200X to 300m in use at end of 200X) with large screens, computing power and keyboards

- Consumer demand for greater mobility and higher personalisation of services, evidenced by the ongoing dramatic impact of Web 2.0 services

- Advertisers' and agencies' desire to reach audiences on their mobiles as traditional advertising channels decline

At the same time, the distribution of digital content to mobile devices has proved extremely challenging for the industry and to date mobile content is essentially the same as that available on personal computers but with a number of drawbacks for consumers who are required to browse in the same way that they would on their PC, but with the limitations of:

- A very small screen

- A restricted User Interface (keyboard, stylus, etc.)

- The need for consistently strong wireless connection

- The relatively high price for the connections required to download the content

- The difficulties in paying for services with credit cards via mobile devices

    Toxic's technology solves many of these problems

3. Target markets & customer offers

Toxic will offer its products and services to four main customer groups. These are:

- **Mobile Consumer Users** – Toxic's technology allows mobile consumers to more easily, quickly and cheaply get access to their preferred content and services via their mobile phone. Consumers download the Toxic software onto their mobile at no cost. They can then add a range of mobile micro applications (apps) which run specific pieces of content, e.g., BBC sports ticker, Reuters stock quotes, train times, etc. Where apps are purchased by consumers, billing can be done via premium SMS capability within the Toxic software thereby eliminating the need to exchange credit card information

- **Advertisers** – The Toxic software contains a permanent advertising banner and advertisements are fed into the consumer's phone. Advertisers, advertising agencies and marketing organisations will be offered the opportunity to display their advertising messages directly on the consumer's mobile device. Through its consumer database of registered consumers, Toxic will be able to offer advertisers well-profiled lists of consumers so that the advertising can be highly targeted and maximise return on investment

- **Software Developers** – Apps can be created by Toxic, third-party software developers or content providers themselves by using the Toxic Software Developer Kit. Toxic will also encourage developers to sell their own Apps

- **Content Providers** – Toxic will offer content providers a way of extending and more closely targeting their reach to mobile consumers. Content providers are seeking ways to expand the reach of their content delivery, particularly through mobile devices and are seeking ways to improve the customer experience. Many content providers generate some or all of their revenue through sales of advertising. Advertising revenues are usually driven directly or indirectly by the number of 'eyeballs'

4. Market overview & competition

The global market for digital mobile content is expanding very rapidly, driven by mobile service providers seeking ways to replace falling voice revenues, the increasing uptake of powerful 'Smartphones' with large screens and high levels of computing power and consumer demand for greater mobility and higher personalisation of services.

Worldwide cellular subscribers are forecasted to reach 3.2 billion by the end of 20XX. Of this, there are already 270m 'Smartphone' users and this number is expected to grow at a rate of 12 per cent p.a. over the same period. The market for mobile content and services is expected to grow dramatically over the next five years, from £85m in 20XX to £280m by 20XX and the market for mobile marketing and advertising is expected to be worth about $3bn by the end of 200X and will rise to $19bn in 20XX.

5. Differentiation & selling points

- Toxic software allows mobile consumers to more easily, quickly and cheaply get access to their preferred content and services via their mobile phone than any other way currently available in the market

- Only the consumers' preferred content from their favourite content providers is delivered and automatically refreshed

- The software is free to the consumer and open to software developers to create new services to appeal to consumers

- Software developers can generate revenues from their efforts

- Digital advertisers can do highly targeted campaigns on mobile phones

- Services are billed via SMS with no need to provide credit card details

- Toxic has developed a compelling User Interface (UI) that enables simple access to mobile content

6. Sales & marketing plans

Sales

Toxic will focus on two main sales channels to enter the market and to build a community of customers. These are:

- Direct/face-to-face sales to content providers – to be done by existing Toxic Directors

- Online channels to software developers – through its own website and other online networks

Over time, it will develop a mixture of sales channels for its client acquisition, retention and development to ensure that it has sufficient market coverage to meet its sales and revenue objectives and to reach the scale required to achieve the long-term operational model. These channels will vary by market segment and customer proposition and will include a mixture of direct, partner and third parties.

Marketing

Toxic will implement a limited but strong integrated marketing communications plan. Some activities are already underway and others will be added once funding is in place.

- Toxic has already created a new brand identity/logo

- At launch, the company will carry out a targeted electronic direct marketing campaign to raise awareness and interest among its prospective customers

- The Toxic website will include a forum for debate and discussion among these target groups and it is envisaged that a community will be created that will share and exchange knowledge around the Toxic proposition as well as spread the word to other developers around the world

- A PR campaign will be undertaken which will target leading online publications

7. Management team

- Thomas Eliot: Founder & Chairman – Over 20 years building businesses and international sales in IT industry. Formerly with Big Telco Ltd and Bigger Mobile Company Ltd

- Anthony Levin: Chief Technical Officer – Designed and developed Toxic's software. Expertise in specification, design and implementation of complex software components gained at Sparky Computers

- Gabby Ratchet: Marketing Director – Gabby brings more than 20 years experience in marketing communications at Retail Leaders Ltd and as MD of her own Clever marketing agency

Full CVs of the management of the company are supplied with this plan.

8. Operational capability

Toxic will require the following operational capability to deliver its proposition:

- Small team of software developers and database administrators – about 4–6, mainly subcontracted

- Hosting and Server capacity – outsourced to third party

- Sales & Marketing team – 2–3 permanent staff

- Website with leading Content Management System and a Content Manager – 1–2 permanent staff

- Billing System/Service – subcontracted to Billing supplier

9. Partnership & supplier arrangements

Toxic will put in place supplier agreements with a number of key partners, including for billing services, customer management/call centre capability and for the supply of SIM cards for use by consumers in their phones. Discussions are well advanced with several of these. Partnerships will be based commercially on revenue-sharing arrangements. A full list of partnership arrangements are provided in an Appendix to this plan.

10. Implementation plan

A separate and detailed implementation plan has been prepared by the company showing the main actions required to launch the business, timescales and responsibilities for each action and risks and how these will be dealt with – this plan is supplied in an Appendix.

11. Financial forecast

The business is highly cash generative, once through its initial 12–18-month start-up phase, and produces gross margins of 90 per cent plus upon reaching its long-term operational model (within two years). In addition, it has low fixed costs and overheads, which give it net profit margins of up to 90 per cent.

Summary Financial Forecast

Profit & Loss	2007	2008	2009	2010
Sales	33,331	551,373	3,793,960	11,417,700
Cost of Goods Sold	(15,764)	(94,884)	(96,508)	(5,597)
Gross Margin	17,567	456,489	3,697,452	11,412,103
Gross Margin (%)	53%	83%	97%	100%
Overheads	135,229	543,472	1,079,823	1,272,745
Net Profit (before tax)	(117,661)	(86,983)	2,617,628	10,139,358
Net Profit (before tax) (%)	-353%	-16%	69%	89%

A separate detailed Financial Forecast showing three-year profit and loss and cashflow forecasts is provided with this plan.

12. Key assumptions

Revenues – Toxic will generate revenues by offering its products and services to four main customer groups.

■ MOBILE CONSUMERS – Where it will provide its

software free of charge once the consumer has registered. Some apps will be charged for and this will generate revenues from consumers

- ADVERTISERS will be offered the opportunity to gain access to a large and well-profiled database of registered users so that they can place targeted advertising via the Toxic system. This will generate advertising revenues

- SOFTWARE DEVELOPERS will be given free access to the Toxic Software Developer Kit, so that they can create services which operate on the Toxic platform, and can benefit from sharing the revenues generated from sales of these to consumers

- CONTENT PROVIDERS will be offered a range of services that use the Toxic system to give consumers access to their content in a simple and low-cost way. This will generate software licensing and services fees

Costs – Costs are based on extensive research carried out with partners and suppliers over the last two years. We have detailed figures available upon request and these are supported by price estimates and quotations from our suppliers. These are shown in an Appendix.

13. Funding requirement & use of funds

The company is currently seeking to raise equity funding of £25,000. This will be used for:

- £10,000 – Sales and marketing – direct and viral marketing, PR, website development and forum management

- £5,000 – Technology/software platform development – porting of services to other operating systems, productisation, product development

- £5,000 – Staff recruitment and training – technical and sales/marketing/account management staff

- £3,000 – New services development
- £2,000 – Working Capital & Contingency – professional fees, equipment, operational costs, contingency

14. Milestones & momentum

Over the last three years, Toxic has been investing to develop its core software platform and to create momentum around its proposition. It is now seeking to scale up rapidly around its management team, competences, propositions and business model. To date, it has:

- Assembled a strong management team

- Established a stable technology platform for delivery of our services to customers

- Created a fully functional demonstrator service (the eBay APP)

- Developed a clearly articulated customer proposition for digital content providers, third-party developers, consumers and advertisers

- Created a new brand identity and formulated a marketing plan

- Developed plans for the immediate recruitment of a full-time CEO, technical staff and sales personnel

15. Main risks

Toxic has identified a number of risks and threats to execution of its strategy and plans. These are set out below along with details of the plans that have been developed to counter these risks and threats.

Threat/Risk	Impact	Defence/Mitigation Strategy
Limited resources (funding, manpower)	Slows speed to market penetration, restricts delivery capability	Timely funding to enable execution of plan
Reaction by the 'big boys' e.g., Nokia, Vodafone	Well funded similar product threatens to swamp us	Make rapid market entry and grab market share while larger players take time
Poor reaction in market place to our concept	Customers denigrate product and adversely impact reputation	Test with customers ahead of launch and refine accordingly

16. Exit strategy

Toxic aims to be acquired within a three–five year timeframe. It has identified a number of potential organisations that could buy it including advertising agencies, mobile telephone service providers and software development companies.

Thomas Eliot – CEO
Toxic Limited 2010

Top tips for writing Business Plans

Developing a good Business Plan can propel you forward in many ways. Among other things it gives you a clear roadmap of where you are going and massively helps your fundraising efforts. So get it right.

1   **Structure** – Find a structure that you like the look of – you can use ours in this book (and can download a template from our website), or something else if you prefer. Whatever this is, make sure the content required in the four main sections outlined above is covered. Ensure that you have a table of contents at the start to guide the reader to where they want to look. Number the pages. Put supporting material in appendices so that it doesn't clog up the main plan

2   **Do It Yourself** – Try to avoid subcontracting or outsourcing the creation of your plan to someone else unless you absolutely have to and then make sure that they work very closely with you. It needs to be your plan and come not only from your head but also from your heart

3   **Keep it Simple** – Don't think that it's a good idea to simply write as much as you can so as to make it look bigger or more impressive. It will have the opposite effect. It's much better to have ten really good pages than fifty of waffle

4   **. . . but Give Enough Detail** – At the same time as not writing reams of rubbish, you need to include enough detailed information to ensure that the reader gets what they need to be able to make an appraisal of your plans. It's not always easy to do this and can take more time, but it is worth it

5   **Get it Reviewed** – When you have a draft of your Business Plan, give it to other people whose opinion you value and trust and ask them for critical feedback on it. If you have one, get your mentor involved in this. Then take on board what they have told you, use your judgement to accept or reject it and revise your plan accordingly

6   **Presentation** – The layout and appearance can have a huge bearing on how your plan is initially received and then judged by the reader. Make it look good and people will pick it up. Make

the layout clear and people will start to read it. Write it well and they will read it all the way through. Try to look at some other people's business plans and borrow good 'look and feel' ideas from those. Include pictures, diagrams and illustrations if these help to bring to life what you propose

7   **Hard Copy** – Print it out to see what it looks like in hard copy. Whoever is reading it will probably do this so make sure you know what it will look like for them when it emerges from their printer. Avoid using anything but True Type fonts that you know will work with any software applications and remember it might be printed in monochrome

8   **Soft Copy** – You will probably be sending it by email to readers so make sure that it's not too large. Try to avoid too many memory-hungry inserts, like photos and pictures that could cause your precious plan to get stuck in the recipient's firewall or bounced into cyberspace – you will want to include some but just be careful. Also, make sure it's in a commonly used software application – stick to MS Word or PDF or something compatible with those and make sure it can be opened by both a Windows-based PC and an Apple Mac

9   **Revamp** – They say that a Business Plan is out of date the moment that you finish it. In fact it's never finished because things change and move on all the time. So don't be afraid to revise as often as you like to reflect these changes. Just give it a different version number and start using that from then on. When you send it to someone ask them to destroy any previous versions that they might have so that there is no confusion later

10   **Numbers** – Make sure that you get this part of the plan right. If you are giving a presentation of your plan ensure that you know off by heart the main numbers for your business, such as your prices, costs, sales and profit margins for each year of the plan. This is an area where whoever is looking at your plan will put some focus and will expect you to have thought about it properly and know what you are doing. Hesitation on your part will imply ignorance leading to a lack of confidence from the audience

11   **Honesty** – Make sure that your plan is as accurate and honest
     as you can be about your business. Nothing that you know to
     be untrue should be in there. If you aren't certain of something
     then you should be telling people that it is an assumption and
     that this is how you came up with it. It's acceptable not to
     know, but unacceptable not to tell the truth

It's a Living Thing

Between us we've read thousands of Business Plans over the course
of our careers. We've also written quite a few. In all the companies
that we've worked in, the plan has changed to varying degrees within
a few weeks of launching, sometimes radically changing the business
objectives. So by definition as soon as you've completed your
dazzling masterpiece it will be out of date and you will be thinking
about revising or even starting a new one. But don't use this as an
excuse not to do one. You should think of it as an organic thing that
will change with your need to survive and thrive as a business.
Business Plans are there as a guide to get you going and to help you
to raise the funds that you need and you should be thinking about
doing an updated version of your plan regularly, particularly as
things change.

When Paul and his colleagues were doing their business planning for
Opta in the late 1990s they created a Business Plan. It said that we
would win all of our business from big companies in the telecoms,
media and technology industries. It said that we would reach a
turnover of £50m in five years. Soon after we got going the 'dotcom
crash' happened and then the devastating events of 9/11. Our target
customers cut their spending on the types of projects that we
specialised in. Our order book dried up and we were forced to make
many of our staff redundant just so that we could balance the books
and remain solvent. It was time to evolve or die – within a few
months we had a new plan. This one said that we were a company
providing services to the public sector. We rehired in one way or
another many of the staff we had laid off. We quickly prospered and
although we never made it to £50m we did well – and a large
US-based company bought us two years later thereby enabling us to
successfully achieve our dream of selling our business.

We were open to rapidly changing our plan even though this meant discarding a lot of thinking, time and energy that we had invested in it. Our survival depended upon evolving, and in so doing we lost some things that we felt were precious to us, but better that than try to hang on to them and thereby become extinct.

NUMBERS

'Carpe Per Diem – Seize the cheque'
Robin Williams

As we said the Business Plan is in two parts – Words and Numbers. Now we will look at the numbers that have to support the words discussed in Chapter 7. So this section looks at how to turn your Business Proposition into a *Business Model* that will describe the way in which you will organise and run your business to make money and create value. It goes on to describe the importance of making a profit and cash and shows you how to put together your Business Model, Profit and Loss and Cashflow Forecasts.

This book is not about accountancy and so we are not going to spend pages trying to explain the finer points of how to calculate profit, the differences between gross and net margins, how to calculate the break-even point and how direct costs differ from fixed costs and overheads. You can find information about all of that in a million places – just google some of those terms and you will see. If you really do want to understand the detail of this, and haven't got the time or inclination to study it for yourself, you should get some professional advice from an accountant. Here we will stick to the basic techniques to help you see if you're making money – and give you a three-step path to follow to achieve this for your business:

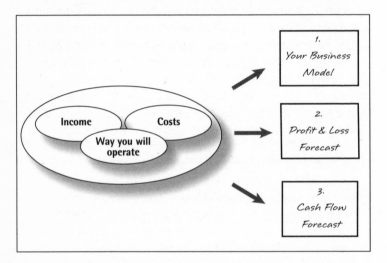

The three steps are:

1   Decide on your simple **Business Model** to show how you will make money from your business

2   Create a **Profit and Loss Forecast** based on your business model to show if it makes money over time

3   Create a **Cashflow Forecast** with money coming in and going out of your business over a given period to show if you will generate enough cash in the business to keep going or if you will need to raise funding to keep you going

1. Building the Business Model

The term Business Model can mean different things to different people and some definitions can make it seem incredibly complicated to understand. What we mean by your Business Model is the way in which your business will operate to make money. You can define your Business Model with the following pieces of information.

Pricing

How and what will your business charge for its products and services: one-off sales, subscriptions, rentals, maintenance charges? Is it a simple product sale where you will charge a one-off amount (e.g., a piece of jewellery), or a subscription service where customers will pay each month or year (mobile phone or cable TV service), or a one-off fee for a service (taxi ride) or a product rental (car hire) or where you will licence the use of something for a licence fee (software)? There are many other pricing approaches that you might be able to think of. And to further complicate matters you could have all sorts of combinations of these so you might sell a product for a fee and then offer a maintenance or support service for an annual subscription (e.g., electrical goods). So what are you going to do?

Some of the most successful businesses have developed ways to generate annually recurring revenues (e.g., insurance) where the product or service simply renew for another period unless the customer does something to stop it or sell longer-term contracts (mobile service providers typically offer eighteen-month contracts now) which generate useful additional revenue and mean that they have fewer new customers to acquire in the following year to achieve their targets.

What price you decide to set is also important – we referred to how to do this in the Business Proposition section of this book. Your price needs to be a balance between charging enough to cover your costs and make a profit and low enough to be acceptable in the market place to your customers.

And remember that if you are going to be charging VAT on your products and services that you will need to factor in the prevailing rate of VAT to your model. The VAT will make your product or service more expensive for the buyer, but you will not be the recipient of the extra money – you will merely be a tax collector for the government and will be passing this on to it at a later stage in your quarterly VAT return.

Sales volumes

How many products or services will your business sell of each product or service at the price you have set? If you are targeting business customers then you may be going for a smaller number of customers each year but with a larger value from each sale. However, if you are aiming at consumers, you will probably need more of them to buy from you but usually at a smaller price per item. There are no hard and fast rules about this but when you put your model together, bear this in mind.

Will you be selling one product or service to each customer or multiple to each and how often will you be able to get a repeat sale? A hairdressing business model might work on the basis of a repeat customer every six weeks for a haircut. But if you have a carpet-fitting business you may only sell to each customer once in ten years.

Cost of sales

What will your business need to spend to make or buy the products or services that it will sell? This is how much it will cost you to either make or buy in each product or service that you sell in a particular time period. These are also known as variable costs, because they will vary with the number of products that you make or buy and should include any costs that can directly be attributed to the product or service. For example, raw materials that you will use to build or make a piece of furniture or jewellery or the price that you paid to a manufacturer for their ready-made goods, such as shoes if you run a shoe shop.

To put your model together you will need to decide if you will be *buying* or *building* your products or services. In other words, are you going to manufacture (build) your own products or obtain them (buy) from another person or company so as to sell them with a mark-up on the price? Or maybe buy some ready-made components and do some of the building yourself? If you're buying, how much will you be paying for the items and where will you be getting them from? If you're building, where will you be buying the raw materials and how much will you be paying? Will you use more than one supplier, will they come from overseas (in which case you need to think about import duties and time delays) and what will the payment schedule be? If you're running a service business this equally applies. You could deliver the service yourself or with your staff (build) or you could hire a contractor or associate to deliver for you (buy).

Fixed costs

Also known as operating costs, these are what your business will need to spend to sell, deliver and support its products and services and to run the day-to-day operation of the business. When you start operating what will you need to put in place to be able to sell to and service your customers? Our hairdresser will probably require a salon with equipment as a minimum – fixed costs will include rent, a rent deposit (get ready for this or it can be a nasty shock when you are asked to part with three months' rent upfront) and expenditure on rates, electricity, water charges, staff and so on. Or they may decide that they will offer their hairdressing services in their customers' homes – a different Business Model to the traditional salon model, but no less acceptable. In this case they will have none of these costs. Many small yoga or Pilates teaching businesses rent space in other people's premises on an hourly basis rather than take on the expense of their own place.

Will you need staff or contractors to deliver your services or will you be doing everything yourself? And don't forget to include your own wages or salary – you need to make sure that you have enough to take care of yourself, within what the business can afford, so that you are fit and healthy to make your business a success.

Sales channels (costs of selling)

How will your business make its sales (direct to customer, indirectly through other companies or both, through a retail outlet, online, offline or both or all of these)? Selling costs merit some special attention because they may be variable (if you pay a commission to someone else only when they sell it) or fixed (if you set up your own sales capability) and this can have a profound impact on your business model. You will need to take into account that the sales channels that you will be using will depend upon the types of customer that you are trying to sell to. Will your business sell to consumers (individuals who will use the goods for their personal use), businesses (where they will be used by people to meet their business needs), or a mixture of both? Often these two groups are known as business to consumer (B2C) and business-to-business (B2B). So are you going to build a B2C or a B2B business or both?

How are you going to sell your product or service? Will you be doing all the sales yourself, or are you going to need to hire a salesperson to do the selling, or a mixture of these? You should do some sales activity yourself, at least in the early stages and preferably throughout the life of your business, so that you get a good feel for what is happening in the market and can keep closely in touch with what your customers are thinking and doing. If you hire people, are you going to take them on full-time, part-time or employ them as freelance contractors who will work for a low rate or even on a commission-only basis? If you are intending to sell your products or services through other organisations, what will these be and what will they expect you to pay them to do this for you? For example, retail sales channels usually require a relatively high percentage of the retail price (typically 30–50 per cent) or work on a commission basis so you will need to factor this cost into your calculations. If you are going to sell online, will this be through your own website, in which case how much will you be spending to set up and run this, or through other organisations' sites, in which case what will they be charging you for this, or a mixture of both? If the latter case applies, you should predict what the proportion of sales between your own and others sites will be, as this will affect your costs too. Decide on what your channels to market are going to be. There are a number available to you and you should select the ones that are appropriate and will be effective with your target customers.

Here are the main sales channels open to you:

- DIRECT — Also known as face-to-face sales, this technique is mostly used by businesses selling higher value products and services that require individual and detailed discussion with the customer and therefore a face-to-face meeting usually at the customer's home or office. Direct selling is the most time-consuming and costly way to sell and should only be used where the value of the goods that you are selling can support this cost. If you employed a direct sales person for £30,000 per year plus their other costs (National Insurance, expenses, travel, etc.) and they could make two sales visits every day of the working year (500 in total), each call would cost you more than £60. You should be thinking that probably only one in every ten new sales visits will bring you a customer — which means that each successful call will be £600. Will the gross margin (not the price, remember) of your product or service that you sell repay that cost and still make you a profit? If not, rethink your channel strategy. You can hire a specialist sales company to do direct selling on your behalf and this may help to keep the cost down, particularly if they work on a commission-only basis. However, it is recommended that if you are doing direct selling, you do this yourself because you will keep control of what is being said to your customers, ensure that the deal is done and be able to receive direct feedback to help you to improve what you do.

  Face-to-face selling is also relevant if you are intending to sell your product through retailers because you will probably need to visit a professional retail buyer to do this. As a consumer, any product that you might buy in a store will have been put there by a business selling its goods through that retailer. This is clearly a great way to have your product put in front of thousands of consumers every day without having to go to them. However, your product will be sitting on a shelf next to your competitor's product and may not be in a good position. You will have only limited control over what happens to your product once it gets into the store and will be required to give the retailer anything between 10 per cent and 60 per cent of the retail price of your product. So factor that into your Business Model and see if you still have a viable business!

■ INDIRECT – This is where you sell your products and services through other businesses, such as agents and resellers, again using the face-to-face approach. Sometimes referred to in business as 'the channel' (although it is no different in status to any other channel out there), this approach reduces your cost of selling because you will pay only a percentage of the sale once a sale happens; in other words it takes all the fixed costs of a salesperson away from you. But if you decide to do this then you will probably give up control of where, how, when and at what price your goods are being sold. You will be at the mercy of other sales people who do not work for you and who may have many other products and services to sell, some of which may be more financially rewarding for them. So they may not be motivated at all to sell yours and you will be sitting back at base wondering why no orders are arriving but really knowing why

■ TELEPHONE – This is where you sell your products and services over the phone. Telesales can be a highly effective way to reach a large number of customers in a short space of time and at relatively low cost. You can either do this yourself, hire someone to do it or subcontract it to another organisation. It can also be useful in generating and qualifying sales leads for direct selling, so that sales people only go to sales visits that have a higher chance of being fruitful. Telesales has something of a bad reputation because a number of organisations have abused it over the years and it can be very tough to do it — there is a high degree of rejection for the sales person who calls and some customers can be abrupt and rude. But it does yield results, particularly if you treat it as a 'numbers game' and don't take it too personally

- ONLINE DIRECT — This is where you sell your goods through your own website. Clearly this is a very fast-growing sales channel. It's simple nowadays to set up your own website and sell your products and services through it. While you will need to pay to get started, usually a few hundred pounds to design and build a website plus the costs of hosting the site, you will be able to keep all the revenues generated for yourself, excluding any credit card charges of course. However, you will need to get people to find you and to come to your site; at least to begin with, finding you will be a little bit like trying to find the proverbial needle in a haystack. So you will inevitably require some marketing spend (such as AdWords or Search Engine Optimisation) as well as finding ways through viral marketing, social networking or other new online marketing techniques to do this

- ONLINE INDIRECT — This is where you sell your products and services through the websites of other businesses. There are many third-party websites where you can sell your goods, many of these specialising in a particular market. If you use household name sites, like for example Kelkoo (for electronic products) or Amazon (originally for books, now a wide range of products) or eBay (for just about anything), you will benefit from having millions of consumers visiting their site (and potentially looking at your goods) every week. But bear in mind that you will be in there with many other products and services, including potentially your competitors, and may be lost in the crowd. The same pros and cons as with selling through third-party bricks and mortar retailers apply here

- DIRECT MAIL – Some would categorise this as marketing rather than selling, but for our purposes this is a useful channel to market that can bring you good sales enquiries and sometimes direct orders. To do this you will need to acquire lists of target customers from the various sources that offer these. You will also need to put together an attractive 'mail piece' – the letter or brochure that you will be sending in order to stimulate a response from the recipient – and this will need to contain some eye-catching offer. The quality of the mailing list and the mail piece has a large bearing on the success of these campaigns, where you can expect to get a 1–3 per cent response rate from those mailed

- ELECTRONIC DIRECT MAIL – This cyberspace version of direct mail has seen a huge growth in recent years and can be effective in the same way as its paper-based namesake. This is less expensive than standard direct mail because you don't need to produce a physical piece, but be careful about how and where you send electronic direct mail as you can upset many by being seen as spam and you may be unwanted

These are the main things that you need to think about when putting together your business model. They are the building blocks of your business and you will need to work out all of these for your particular business in order to put your model together. Get the basics of your Business Model – the way in which you are going to operate to make money – sorted out and you will start to see if it looks like you have something that will fly. By doing this you may start to pick up things that don't work. You can then take a look at each of the building blocks in turn to see if you can make adjustments to the model, for example, raise your price, sell more, use a different sales channel, reduce your fixed costs, etc.

As an example, let's turn to our old friends Styx Jewellery again. These are the key elements of its business model:

- *PRICING – The business makes a range of five jewellery products. Each product has a different price, ranging from £80 to £400 to the consumer*

- *SALES VOLUMES – The business aims to sell a total of 62 pieces in its first month of trading and then gradually increase its volumes to a peak of 114 per month after 8 months*

- *COST OF SALES – Each product has a different cost of sale – the cost to make each product, ranging from £50 to £250 per product*

- *FIXED COSTS – The business rents a small premises that doubles as workshop and office. It employs one person to make the jewellery and run the business, and also runs a website through which it sells its products*

- *SALES CHANNELS AND SELLING COSTS – Once the website is up and running there is little cost of selling except for hosting fees, postage and the 2–4 per cent credit card charge*

Now think about your own Business Model using this approach.

Forecasting

A key part of your planning involves putting together a projection of what income will be generated by your business and how you expect to pay for everything you need to enable to make your business function. Only when you have done these forecasts will you know whether or not you have a potentially viable business, and whether you can make money from it. They will also provide you with ideas about what you might need to change (such as higher price, more sales, less costs) to make your Business Model work. You cannot, therefore, set off on your journey without it.

This projection is known as your Financial Forecast and forms the Numbers section of your Business Plan. You will need to make a well-informed prediction of what you expect your business to sell and to spend over a period of time, typically the first two or three years of your business. The figures that you use will need to be backed up with an explanation – a set of assumptions – of why you have used those figures.

Financial Forecasts deal with two main areas:

■ *INCOME – What money you expect to bring into the business through sales of your products and services to customers as well as any other finance which you might raise through bank loans, overdrafts, selling shares to investors or grants*

■ *EXPENDITURE – What money you expect to go out of the business to pay for everything you require to make or buy your products and services as well as all the costs of running the business like wages, premises, running costs and other expenses. It should include everything that you can foresee coming in and going out, with no exceptions*

Often the difficulty in putting together a forecast, and the reason why some people feel the urge to put it aside and hope that it will go away and that they won't have to do it, lies in two things: how to structure and present this information and where to find the information. But once you know what you're doing, this is once again relatively straightforward. We'll come on to those two things shortly.

Whether you are comfortable dealing with numbers or not, how you think your business will perform financially is central to being successful and in getting others to support you. By numbers we are not talking about complicated maths, more like simple arithmetic: if you can add, subtract, multiply and divide then you have got all the basic skills required to execute the method that we will show you here. In fact if you don't possess the ability to complete simple arithmetic then you should be asking yourself if being in business is really right for you because you will be using it every day and it's a critical skill to possess. But if you really are struggling to do this, don't worry – you are not alone. There are lots of people and organisations who can help you – go to www.whatsyourbrightidea. biz where you will find a list of possible places to find help. But remember, whether you do it yourself or get help, this must be done!

If you're looking for funding to get you started then a forecast is an essential part of your business plan – potential lenders or investors will be looking at this to see how you will make your business viable. If they decide to invest, how will you provide them with a return on their investment so that they will get their money back and will get an additional sum, be it interest on a loan or a lump sum if you sell the company, to reward them for the risk that they have taken to help you get started? It's back to the simple risk–reward equation: they are taking a risk with their money and will want a reward for taking that risk. Different types of investors will be seeking different amounts of return on their investment. We will cover the sorts of returns that different types of investors will be looking for later in this book.

How to forecast

To those who have never done it, putting together a Financial Forecast may at first appear daunting. Most people have some idea about how their revenue figures will be made up – they can make an estimate about how many sales they are going to make and at what price they will make them. As far as costs go, most will also have an idea about some of the costs they will incur, though usually not all of them. But how do you structure the forecast, where do you get the information from and what about when you really have little idea about the costs of things because it's just too early to predict this? These are the common issues that face everyone when doing their forecast, even in large and well-established businesses.

It's important to get the forecast as accurate as you can because you will be using it as the basis for decisions that you will make to run the business – how much you will be able to pay for goods, pay staff, rent premises, spend on IT equipment and so on. Getting it wrong could mean that you run out of money before you even get started and that could spell the end of the business. Also, once again it's better to discover at this planning stage whether or not you think the business can be viable, rather than unhappily finding this out later when you have committed even more time and expense to it. By doing this forecast you will start to see what you can afford, how many sales you will need to make, where you need to do things differently to make your business case work. So think of it as a planning tool to help you make decisions on some of these things.

You can get all you need into a two-page Financial Forecast – one for your Profit and Loss Forecast and one for your Cashflow Forecast. Not reams and reams of spreadsheets full of complicated figures, just two pages with the essential information.

2. Profit and Loss Forecast

Before we get into the Profit and Loss Forecast we need to explain the fundamentals of profit and why it is important.

In business there is one golden rule. However you do it, your business must bring in more money than it spends. Put simply, Profit – the bottom line – is the difference between the money that your business earns, principally by selling products and services to your customers, and the money that goes out of your business to buy or make the things that you sell as well as to cover all of your operating costs. We'll come on to how you calculate profit shortly but in simple terms profit can be expressed as:

$$Profit = Income - Costs$$

The objective is to get more in than you let go out. In many cases it is unlikely that you will make a profit to begin with because it will take you time to build up sales and you will need to incur some costs to get started. However, a failure to achieve profit over time will mean that you will not be in business for very long unless you can find a benefactor who will inject money into your business to keep you afloat. But usually this comes at a price unless you are very fortunate.

While business can allow you to do many things, including create jobs, innovate, improve people's lives and help society, making profit remains paramount. It is often said that you can't make a profit unless you make a difference but also that you can't make a difference unless you make a profit. This applies even with social businesses, where profit may be seen by some as somewhat secondary to the worthy aims of the business. In these cases you should think of it as profit to sustain the business and as a key contributor to reinvestment in the business.

Outside of this simple equation shown above, one that we should all understand in our personal financial life as well (we hope), everything else that you will do in your business can be thought of as a means to that end. You might say it's the necessary evil that has to be gone through to achieve the desired outcome. Whatever you choose to do with your time, money and other resources while running your business, however fun or worthy or interesting or inspiring they might be, the focus must be on making that profit.

How to do a Profit and Loss Forecast

The Profit and Loss Forecast shows if your business is likely to operate profitably or at a loss. A profit and loss forecast needs to show performance over a period of time in order to give a realistic picture of what's happening financially in the business. Just doing it for one or two months can give a false picture. For example, as you may be investing at the beginning with sales only coming through later. In its simplest form it's made up of the following elements:

A		B		C		D		E
Income	–	Cost of Goods	=	Gross Profit	–	Fixed Costs	=	Net Profit

We have already seen what the terms Income, Cost of Goods and Fixed Costs mean. In addition, the terms Gross and Net Profit need to be understood.

■ *GROSS PROFIT – Also known as Gross Margin. This is the difference between the income that you* receive for each of your products or services and what it costs you to make or buy each one. For example, if you design and sell T-shirts for £40 and the raw materials (plain T-shirt, dyes, transfers, printing costs) are £20 for each shirt then your gross profit will be £20

■ NET PROFIT – Also known as Net Margin or Earnings or Operating Profit. This is 'the bottom line' that we referred to earlier. It is the difference between your gross profit (the profit on all products and services) and all your fixed costs for your business. So if you sold 100 T-shirts at a gross profit of £20 you would make £2,000 gross profit. If your fixed costs were then, say, £1,500 for the year you would make a net profit of £500

So now you can put a Profit and Loss Forecast together. As an example we return to Styx Jewellery, a small business making a range of jewellery products that it sells through its own website. The following illustrates how profit is simply calculated over a three-month period – you should do your forecast over an initial twelve months, and preferably for two–three years. The example uses the formula that we showed earlier:

Styx Profit and Loss Forecast – first three months

		April	May	June	Total (A/M/J)
A	**Income** (also called Turnover or Revenue or Sales)	£8,000	£11,000	£12,000	**£31,000**
B	**Cost of Goods** (what it cost you to buy or make the products or services that you sold)	£5,000	£4,500	£4,500	**£14,000**
C	**Gross Profit** A–B	£3,000	£6,500	£7,500	**£17,000**
D	**Fixed Costs** (All other expenditure made to run your business). For example:				
	Website	£5,000	£0	£0	£5,000
	Staff Wages	£3,800	£3,800	£3,800	£11,400
	Premises Rental	£1,000	£1,000	£1,000	£3,000
	Telephones/Broadband	£100	£100	£100	£300
	Electricity/Gas	£50	£50	£50	£150
	Business Rates	£200	£200	£200	£600
	Insurance	£100	£100	£100	£300
	TOTAL OTHER COSTS	£10,250	£5,250	£5,250	£20,750
E	**Net Profit** C–D	**-£7,250**	**£1,250**	**£2,250**	**-£3,750**

As we can see the business has made a loss in its first month and even though it has made profits in the next two months, overall for a three-month period it has made a loss of £3,750. However, this serves to illustrate why a profit and loss account needs to be compiled for a longer period of time. Take a look at the same profit and loss for a full twelve-month period. As you can see, over a full year Styx is forecasting to make a healthy profit of £48,450 on income of £167,000.

Your business levers

Once you have put together your Profit and Loss Forecast you will build up a picture of how you think your business is going to perform financially over a period of time. If it's making a profit that's all well and good, but what about if it shows you that you are making a loss or too small a profit to make your efforts worthwhile? Now you can use the forecast as a tool to play with some of the assumptions that you have made to see if you can get it to work financially.

Any business has a number of 'levers' that can be pulled to change the financial performance. These levers are the elements of your Business Model that we detailed above but in summary they are:

- Pricing
- Sales Volumes
- Cost of Sales
- Fixed Costs
- Sales Channels and Selling Costs

Playing with these elements to find the best approach for you can be a fascinating and rewarding part of planning your business. You can, and should, always be looking for opportunities to reshape the way you do these things – there is potential to make more money if you think it through carefully.

For example, with pricing you can put up your prices by say, 10 per cent, and this will have a marked effect on your income. Simple, you may think – do this and keep all my costs the same and profits will

Styx Jewellery – Profit and Loss Forecast (year one)

	April Plan	May Plan	June Plan	July Plan	Aug Plan	Sept Plan	Oct Plan	Nov Plan	Dec Plan	Jan Plan	Feb Plan	Mar Plan	Total Plan
Sales													
Necklace	1,600	2,200	2,400	2,600	2,800	2,800	3,000	3,200	3,200	3,200	3,200	3,200	33,400
Bracelet	1,600	2,200	2,400	2,600	2,800	2,800	3,000	3,200	3,200	3,200	3,200	3,200	33,400
Earrings	1,600	2,200	2,400	2,600	2,800	2,800	3,000	3,200	3,200	3,200	3,200	3,200	33,400
Rings	1,600	2,200	2,400	2,600	2,800	2,800	3,000	3,200	3,200	3,200	3,200	3,200	33,400
Brooches	1,600	2,200	2,400	2,600	2,800	2,800	3,000	3,200	3,200	3,200	3,200	3,200	33,400
TOTAL INCOME	**8,000**	**11,000**	**12,000**	**13,000**	**14,000**	**14,000**	**15,000**	**16,000**	**16,000**	**16,000**	**16,000**	**16,000**	**167,000**
Cost of Sales													
Necklace	1,000	900	900	900	800	800	800	800	800	800	800	800	10,100
Bracelet	1,000	900	900	900	800	800	800	801	801	801	801	801	10,105
Earrings	1,000	900	900	900	800	800	800	802	802	802	802	802	10,110
Rings	1,000	900	900	900	800	800	800	803	803	803	803	803	10,115
Brooches	1,000	900	900	900	800	800	800	804	804	804	804	804	10,120
TOTAL COST OF SALES	**5,000**	**4,500**	**4,500**	**4,500**	**4,000**	**4,000**	**4,000**	**4,010**	**4,010**	**4,010**	**4,010**	**4,010**	**50,550**
Gross Profit	**3,000**	**6,500**	**7,500**	**8,500**	**10,000**	**10,000**	**11,000**	**11,990**	**11,990**	**11,990**	**11,990**	**11,990**	**116,450**
Gross Profit as a % of Sales	38%	59%	63%	65%	71%	71%	73%	75%	75%	75%	75%	75%	70%
Overheads													
Website	5,000	–	–	–	–	–	–	–	–	–	–	–	5,000
Wages/Salaries (net pay)	3,000	3,000	3,000	3,000	3,000	3,000	3,000	3,000	3,000	3,000	3,000	3,000	36,000
National Insurance/ (PAYE)	800	800	800	800	800	800	800	800	800	800	800	800	9,600
Premises Rent	1,000	1,000	1,000	1,000	1,000	1,000	1,000	1,000	1,000	1,000	1,000	1,000	12,000
Telephone/Broadband	100	100	100	100	100	100	100	100	100	100	100	100	1,200
Electricity/Gas	50	50	50	50	50	50	50	50	50	50	50	50	600
Business Rates	200	200	200	200	200	200	200	200	200	200	200	200	2,400
Insurance	100	100	100	100	100	100	100	100	100	100	100	100	1,200
TOTAL OVERHEADS	**10,250**	**5,250**	**5,250**	**5,250**	**5,250**	**5,250**	**5,250**	**5,250**	**5,250**	**5,250**	**5,250**	**5,250**	**68,000**
Net Profit	**-7,250**	**1,250**	**2,250**	**3,250**	**4,750**	**4,750**	**5,750**	**6,740**	**6,740**	**6,740**	**6,740**	**6,740**	**48,450**
Net Profit as a % of Sales	-91%	11%	19%	25%	34%	34%	38%	42%	42%	42%	42%	42%	29%

increase. But what about the impact of putting prices up by 10 per cent: will customers still buy from you when they can probably go to a competitor for a lower price? You will need to make sure that you are offering something better to justify the higher price or it's doubtful that customers will buy from you.

With cost of sales, how about getting your suppliers to drop the price at which you buy raw materials from them? That's a good idea, but they may be unwilling to do this unless you buy in bulk, which would then mean that you would need more cash to finance it. And how realistic is this anyway?

With channels to market, what about selling only online rather than selling to bricks and mortar retail stores? This will reduce your selling costs dramatically, but will you reach enough customers this way? Also bear in mind that the market will probably have an expectation of how they buy your types of product or service from what's already available in the market so there may not always be scope for doing things differently. A hairdresser may be able to persuade some customers to have their hair done at home but many will want the experience of going to a professional salon and all that goes with it. So is there scope to reduce the operating costs by not paying for premises? That may be so, but this would probably then have an impact on the number of clients that they could see each week because of travelling time. This could lead to a reduction in income and would generate some travelling costs.

So if you want to change the rules of the game by modelling your offer differently, think carefully about how customers might behave towards you if you do. Imagine if a bank had come to you in the 1980s and said that you could only do business with them by phone or over the Internet, you might have given them a funny look, but this is commonplace now because they managed to change the Business Model.

3. Cashflow Forecast

Before we get into explaining how to put together a Cashflow Forecast we first need to set out why cashflow is so important.

Did we say that there is nothing more important in business than profit? This is true, but many would argue that in practical terms there is another measure of financial performance that is equally important and one that you ignore at your peril. This is Cash. Cash is the lifeblood of your business and it's important to understand the difference between profit and cash.

As we showed with the simple equation above, profit is the difference between the *income* (i.e., sales, revenues, turnover) received by your business and all its *costs* (i.e., expenditure, expenses, overheads) over a period of time. Profit is typically calculated and displayed in a profit and loss account, a table that shows everything that came into your business and everything that went out with the difference between the two totals being the profit (if a positive number) or loss (if a negative number). Straightforward. But what the profit and loss account does not accurately show is exactly when the money arrived in your bank account or went out of it. So you might think that you are doing well and making a profit but if you haven't been paid by your customer or have had to make an outlay for stock or services yourself, then you may be out of cash and insolvent.

So how can we know accurately at any given point how we are doing financially? Cash, or to put it more correctly, 'cashflow', shows your actual financial position. Cash includes notes and coins, the money in your easy-access bank accounts, your bank overdraft facility (if you have one) and any other sources of money that you can quickly get your hands on. It does not include amounts in the bank that you cannot access quickly, like money owed by your customers or money tied up in goods that you have not yet sold (i.e., stock). If you are receiving more cash than you are spending at any given point then your business will be *cashflow positive*; if you are spending more than you are receiving you will be *cashflow negative*.

How to do a Cashflow Forecast

Your Cashflow Forecast will contain the same revenues and most of the costs as your Profit and Loss Forecast. However, you will organise them so that they reflect the exact timing of when the money from your sales physically came in and money actually went out of your business bank account, which, as we said before, may be different from how it appears in the Profit and Loss Forecast. So, returning to our styx jewellery example:

Styx Cashflow Forecast – first three months

		April	May	June
A	**Opening Balance** (bank balance at start of month)	£1,000	-£4,975	-£6,200
	Receipts (Income from)			
	Sales	£7,000	£9,000	£11,000
	VAT	£1,225	£1,575	£1,925
B	**TOTAL RECEIPTS**	£8,225	£10,575	£12,925
	Payments (Outgoings for)			
	Raw Materials	£5,900	£3,000	£4,000
	Staff Wages	£3,800	£3,800	£3,800
	Premises Rental	£3,000	–	–
	Telephones/Broadband	£300	–	–
	Electricity/Gas	–	–	£150
	VAT Payments	–	–	–
	Business Rates	£1,200	–	£4,725
	Insurance £600			
C	**TOTAL PAYMENTS**	£14,200	£6,800	£13,275
D	**Closing Balance** (bank balance at end of month) A + B – C	-£4,975	-£6,200	£11,550

In this example, Styx forecasts that it will start its first month of trading with £1,000 in the bank. It predicts that it will receive £8,225 in income from sales, including the VAT that it will charge its customers as part of the sale price. It will spend £14,200 in the first month on a range of things needed to make its products and run the business. If it operated its business along these lines it would have a closing bank balance at the end of the month of minus £4,975. The closing bank balance at the end of the month becomes the opening balance at the start of the next month and the income and expenditure process is repeated for that month and so on. Clearly, this forecast shows that Styx has an unsustainable cashflow position for the first two months of operation; unless it can find funds to cover its negative bank balance it would be out of business. It simply runs out of money before it can even get going.

Remember, this is just a forecast. By doing this forecast before starting trading the owners of Styx can now see the amount of funding that they will require to allow them to operate the business until it starts to generate enough income to become cashflow positive.

Now take a look at the cashflow position for Styx Jewellery shown on the next two pages. Styx plans to start trading in April and its management has put together a Cashflow Forecast for the first twelve months of the company's existence.

As you can see in Example 1, while the business is doing well by generating a consistent flow of sales income, it predicts that it will spend more on its overhead costs in the first six months than it will receive in income – cashflow negative. But after six months it will start to make more money than it will spend – cashflow positive. So to get it to the position where it is cashflow positive it will either need to do better at sales, reduce its costs or fill the funding gap with an injection of cash, i.e., a loan or cash in return for shares in the business.

In Example 2 the funding gap has been filled for the period required. In this case, the owners have raised £12,000 in equity (they will have given up a share of the business to gain this) and a £2,000 bank loan. Notice that even this amount is not enough to keep the business in the black in the months of June and July – but they are able to bridge this period by using the overdraft that they agreed with their bank.

1. Styx Cashflow Forecast

1 — You can do this for each day, week, month, quarter – here it's by month. Choose your time period

2 — Amount in your bank account at start of the period

3 — All money received into your bank account during the month

4 — All money paid out of your bank account during the month

5 — What's left in the bank at the end of the month

6 — If you have an overdraft facility you can include this in your calculation

7 — What's left in the bank at the end of the month including using your overdraft

These are the key lines – if it is a negative number at the end of the month then you will need to inject funds into the business to make it a positive. Otherwise you are insolvent and out of business.

	April	May	June	July	Aug	Sept	Oct	Nov	Dec	Jan	Feb	Mar
						2010						
Opening Balance	1,000	-4,975	-6,200	-11,550	-11,375	-7,725	-12,000	-10,475	-4,475	-6,450	-3,750	2,250
Receipts												
Cash from Sales	7,000	8,000	8,000	9,000	10,000	10,000	11,000	12,000	12,000	12,000	12,000	12,000
Cash from Debtors	–	1,000	3,000	4,000	4,000	4,000	4,000	4,000	4,000	4,000	4,000	4,000
VAT	1,225	1,575	1,925	2,275	2,450	2,450	2,625	2,800	2,800	2,800	2,800	2,800
Other Receipts	–	–	–	1,000	–	–	–	–	1,000	–	–	–
Sales of Assets	–	–	–	–	–	–	–	–	–	–	–	–
Capital Investment Introduced	–	–	–	–	–	–	–	–	–	–	–	–
Loans Introduced	–	–	–	–	–	–	–	–	–	–	–	–
TOTAL RECEIPTS	8,225	10,575	12,925	16,275	16,450	16,450	17,625	18,800	19,800	18,800	18,800	18,800
Payments												
Raw Materials	5,900	3,000	4,000	4,000	4,000	4,000	4,000	4,000	4,000	4,000	4,000	4,000
Wages/Salaries (net pay)	3,000	3,000	3,000	3,000	3,000	3,000	3,000	3,000	3,000	3,000	3,000	3,000
National Insurance/PAYE	800	800	800	800	800	800	800	800	800	800	800	800
Premises Rent	3,000	–	–	3,000	–	–	3,000	–	–	3,000	–	–
Telephone/Broadband	300	–	–	300	–	–	300	–	–	300	–	–
Electricity & Gas	–	–	150	–	–	150	–	–	150	–	–	150
VAT Payments	–	–	4,725	–	–	7,175	–	–	8,225	–	–	8,400
Rates	–	–	600	–	–	600	–	–	600	–	–	600
Insurance	–	–	–	–	–	–	–	–	–	–	–	–
Interest on Loans	1,200	–	–	–	–	–	–	–	–	–	–	–
TOTAL PAYMENTS	8,225	10,575	12,925	16,275	16,450	16,450	17,625	18,800	19,800	18,800	18,800	18,800
Closing Balance	-4,975	-6,200	-11,550	-11,375	-7,725	-12,000	-10,475	-4,475	-6,450	-3,750	2,250	-900
OVERDRAFT FACILITY	5,000	5,000	5,000	5,000	5,000	5,000	5,000	5,000	5,000	5,000	5,000	5,000
Closing Balance – using overdraft	25	-1,200	-6,550	-6,375	-2,725	-7,000	-5,475	525	-1,450	1,250	7,250	4,100

2. Styx Cashflow Forecast – bridging the funding gap

1 Using the same income and costs as in the previous example but ...

2 An investment is made by the owners of the business

3 ... and the owners get a bank loan that will be repaid monthly

4 Ensuring that if the forecast is achieved the business will be comfortably 'in the black' and be able to continue trading

	Year 1											
	April	May	June	July	Aug	Sept	Oct	Nov	Dec	Jan	Feb	Mar
Opening Balance	1,000	5,933	4,617	-825	-724	2,817	-550	883	6,792	4,725	7,333	13,242
Receipts												
Cash from Sales	7,000	8,000	8,000	9,000	10,000	10,000	11,000	12,000	12,000	12,000	12,000	12,000
Cash from Debtors	–	1,000	3,000	4,000	4,000	4,000	4,000	4,000	4,000	4,000	4,000	4,000
VAT (net receipts)	1,225	1,575	1,925	2,275	2,450	2,620	2,625	2,625	2,800	2,800	2,800	2,800
Other Receipts	–	–	–	1,000	–	–	–	–	1,000	–	–	–
Sales of Assets	–	–	–	–	–	–	–	–	–	–	–	–
Capital Investment Introduced	9,000	–	–	–	–	–	–	–	–	–	–	–
Loans Introduced	2,000	–	–	–	–	–	–	–	–	–	–	–
TOTAL RECEIPTS	19,225	10,575	12,925	16,275	16,450	17,625	17,625	18,800	19,800	18,800	18,800	18,800
Payments												
Raw Materials	5,900	3,000	4,000	4,000	4,000	4,000	4,000	4,000	4,000	4,000	4,000	4,000
Wages/Salaries (net pay)	3,000	3,000	3,000	3,000	3,000	3,000	3,000	3,000	3,000	3,000	3,000	3,000
National Insurance/PAYE	800	800	800	800	800	800	800	800	800	800	800	800
Premises Rent	3,000	–	–	3,000	–	–	3,000	–	–	3,000	–	–
Telephone/Broadband	300	–	150	300	–	150	300	–	150	300	–	150
Electricity & Gas	–	–	–	–	–	–	–	–	–	–	–	–
VAT Payments	–	–	4,725	–	–	7,350	–	–	8,225	–	–	8,400
Rates	–	–	600	–	–	600	–	–	600	–	–	600
Insurance	1,200	–	–	–	–	–	–	–	–	–	–	–
Loan Repayments	83	83	83	83	83	83	83	83	83	83	83	83
Interest on Loans	8	8	8	8	8	8	8	8	8	8	8	8
Corporation Tax	–	–	–	–	–	–	–	–	–	–	–	–
TOTAL PAYMENTS	14,292	6,892	13,367	11,192	7,892	15,992	11,192	7,892	16,867	11,192	7,892	17,042
Closing Balance	5,933	4,617	-825	-742	2,817	-550	883	6,792	4,725	7,333	13,242	10,000
OVERDRAFT FACILITY	5,000	5,000	5,000	5,000	5,000	5,000	5,000	5,000	5,000	5,000	5,000	5,000
Closing Balance – using overdraft	10,933	9,617	4,175	4,258	7,817	4,450	5,883	11,792	9,725	12,333	18,242	15,000

The difference between profit and cash

This is a really important distinction to be able to understand. As an example of the difference, in profit terms, we know that if you make or buy an item for £100 and then sell it for £200 you make a £100 gross profit. But what about if you asked the buyer of your product to pay you in 60 or 90 days' time, or they were late paying your invoice? You can still be showing a profit in your Profit and Loss Account but what about the wages, premises rent, electricity and telephone bills that you will have to pay during those two to three months? Unless you can find some other source of funds, you will not have the cash to cover these costs even though you made a profit. And you will probably be out of business.

So profit is only looking at revenues coming into your business and expenditure going out over a period of time from an accountant's point of view. It's important because you will be required to report to the tax authorities in profit and loss terms. But the cash is a much more realistic way of looking at how your business is doing financially: as it looks at the actual movement of money in and out and exactly when this movement occurs, it's a very good way of understanding how you are performing and gives you a very real-time view of whether you are prospering, just surviving or in danger of going under. Unless you have enough cash in your business you will not be able to continue for very long – not without the need to raise funding to bridge any gaps between money going out and income from sales. Imagine the cashflow is just like your own personal bank account. If there is nothing in it you can't pay your bills and you probably need to use a credit facility to bridge the gap.

To continue trading, and to be able to grow your business, you should ideally build up a *cash balance* by ensuring that the timing of cash movements puts you in a positive cashflow situation. Once you get started, if you do not need to use your cash balance immediately, you should consider putting spare cash into an account where it will earn a higher rate of interest. Alternatively, use it to reinvest into your business if you believe it will give you a higher rate of return than in the bank account.

Most experts agree that cash is as important, if not more important, a measure of how your business is doing than profit. You will frequently hear that 'Cash is King' from just about anyone who knows a good business cliché – and they are right. It's also been said that 'you don't spend profit, but you do spend cash'. If you manage your business primarily from a cash perspective, and try to keep it cash positive and build up a cash reserve, you will not go far wrong.

The Balance Sheet

When doing your financial forecasting, you may also be required to provide a third page – a Balance Sheet. This gives a picture of the assets and liabilities that your business has at a given point in time. Some will advise you to put together a balance sheet forecast but our experience is that if you are at the initial stage of setting up a business you do not need to do this. Very early-stage businesses can be understood financially by looking at the Profit and Loss Account, cashflow and your bank statement. Balance sheets show a ledger of assets and liabilities, neither of which you are likely to have to any extent in your early days. Also, if you are intending to set up as a Sole Trader or a general partnership you are not required to produce a Balance Sheet with your annual accounts. If a potential investor or lender really must have one of these we would suggest that you firstly, and politely, ask why this is required (with your inference being that you do not believe it to be necessary at all for a start-up/early stage business); failing that, contact an adviser, such as an accountant, or your mentor or a business support organisation, to help you with it.

Forecast duration?

You will need to decide the duration over which your Profit and Loss and Cashflow Forecasts will run. The intended reader should dictate the duration of your forecast so you may need to do slightly different versions if you want to approach different audiences. For example, a bank might want a three-year forecast but a venture capital company might in some cases ask for four or five years. So find out first what they are looking for before you waste time doing something that is not required. Our view is that any longer than three years into the future is in the realms of science fiction – entertaining and potentially exciting but unlikely to have any impact during your lifetime. For a start-up company, it will be surprising if someone really wants more than three years.

When you compile your forecast, get as accurate a picture as you can for the first year then do your best after that. How much information you will need to include will also vary depending upon the amount of funds you are seeking and the potential source of funding. Typically, the larger the amount the more information required; the opposite case applies with smaller amounts. While this book is mainly concerned with start-up and early stage businesses, the same principles will apply even if you are looking for several millions of pounds. Ultimately, the most important period for your business will be the first twelve months, so make sure that you forecast for that period as a minimum, particularly for cashflow.

Making assumptions

Your financial forecast is only as good as the 'Assumptions' that you use to compile it. So what are these assumptions? If you are doing a forecast for a new business where you have no history or experience of what your likely revenues or costs are going to be, then you need to make a guess – an educated guess and one that is supported by how you came to that conclusion. You will need to be able to show your workings. Don't be frightened to get it wrong to start with – everybody does. Just have a go at filling in the numbers that you have some idea of and then complete the rest of the table with your best guess of what you expect will happen. Then start trying to find better information to revise and refine your forecast as you go along.

Assumptions are an integral part of financial forecasting – without them no one would ever be able to put a forecast together because there will always be some costs that you don't know and predicting accurately what your sales will be is almost impossible.

Tips for financial forecasting

You need to put together a carefully thought-through Financial Forecast to show potential investors or funders that you have a credible plan and to give you a budget to manage the business. So get it right.

■ *GOOD ASSUMPTIONS – Make sure that your assumptions are well reasoned and supported with* evidence – be able to convincingly explain how you came up with each number in your forecast. Don't labour over being too detailed – trying to find the cost of each paperclip or the price of a kilowatt-hour of electricity. But don't make your assumptions too general either so that they become meaningless. Get the balance right

- **BE CONSERVATIVE** – Make your income forecasts reasonable. Most people overestimate the amount of sales that they will make and the speed at which they will achieve them. It always takes longer to achieve your sales than you think, so scale it back to sensible levels and you will look more convincing in investors' eyes and won't set yourself unachievable targets

- **BE LIBERAL** – Overestimate your cost forecasts. Conversely, costs usually turn out to be higher than you thought they would be and occur quicker than you expected, so factor in more

- **FOUR SEASONS** – Take account of seasonality. Many businesses have steady sales throughout the year but some can be 'lumpy'. Does your business have variable sales, like Christmas cards, fireworks, ice cream and garden furniture?

- **REFINE IT** – Always be looking to develop and refine your forecasts as you get better information and learn more. Try to find ways to go out into the real world and negotiate better pricing on things that you buy and feed that into your forecast

- **TAKE YOUR TIME** – Rushed forecasts are usually wrong forecasts. Get a first draft quickly for yourself and be aware of which assumptions are the weakest and where you need to find out more. Then take the time to populate it with the best figures that you can

- **SANITY CHECK** – Ensure that you get someone to review it for you. It's easy even for experienced business people to make simple errors of calculation in spreadsheet formulae that can have a big impact on what you produce. Your mentor would be a good person for this

- **BEWARE SPREADSHEETS** – Don't get caught up in letting the spreadsheet decide what your forecast will come up with. Make sure that you use it as a tool that you control, rather than letting it control you

- **INCREMENTALISM** – Don't get caught in the 'incremental' trap. This is where month on month your sales will grow by 10 or 20 per cent. Tim did this for his first business and was pretty pleased with himself – in three years his sales indicated that the business would reach an income of several million pounds, until Paul pointed out that he would need more stores than actually existed in England to reach the unrealistic target. Ooops! Flattering yourself with pretty spreadsheet predictions is a short-lived joy whereas achieving a realistic target is a much better feeling

BUSINESS STRUCTURE

'Rules are for the obedience of fools and the guidance of wise men.' Douglas Bader

So now we have mapped out how to put your Business Model together and how to compile a financial forecast based on this. In this section we set out the main types of business vehicle or structure that you can choose to operate in and explain the implications for you of each approach. We set out the basic steps to take to get set up and the important rules and regulations that you will need to follow to keep in line with the law, understand your tax position and be a credible business in the eyes of your customers, suppliers and staff.

There is no right or wrong answer to the question 'what type of business vehicle do I set up?' Your choice will be driven by a number of factors including your business objectives, what works best for your business from a financial and tax perspective, how you want to be seen in the market place by your customers, what your competitors do and, to some extent, by your personal financial situation and how you can best optimise this.

The illustration below shows most of the main possible business structures available to you as a new business owner. Clearly it would take an entire book to go into detail for all of these and there are many sources of information available to help you with this.

The range of business structure options

The vast majority of new business owners in the UK set up as either a Sole Trader, Partnership or as a Limited Company. Of the 4.8m small businesses in the UK today, 1.15m are limited companies, 2.8m sole traders and 500,000 partnerships.[3] These three categories account for 94 per cent of all small businesses. Our experience is entirely in line with this in that every business we have worked with over the last twenty-five years has been in one or other of these categories. So for the sake of practicality and simplicity we would recommend that you start off as either a sole trader (if you are intending to work alone), a partnership (if you are intending to work with a few other people of equal status in the business with you) or a limited company. Therefore we focus on these three categories in this book. Remember, you can always start off as a sole trader or partnership and change to a limited company as you grow, although you should think this through carefully before you start, as there can be some issues that need to be addressed.

Whatever structure you decide upon, each has a number of different aspects that you will need to consider. These include what you need

---

3 FSB Small Busines Guide 2010

to do to set up, the legal requirements of each, how and when you will be required to report to government bodies and when you need to submit accounts. And in each case there are a number of advantages and disadvantages.

1. Sole Trader

What is it?

This is the most common form of ownership in the UK and is the simplest way to set up a small business. If you decide to set up as a sole trader (also known as a sole proprietor) then the business will be totally owned by you. You can employ additional people but they will have no ownership of the business. All profits after tax will go to you and similarly all the assets of the business will be owned by you. By the same token, any debts of the business will be your debts and you will be required to find the money personally in order to pay them. This means that you as the owner of a sole trader business will have unlimited liability so your home or other personal assets may be at risk if your business runs into trouble and you have to pay its debts.

Setting up

As a sole trader you can just start trading at any time and can do business under your own name, e.g., Mark Hall Associates or make up a trade name under which you will do business, e.g., Styx Enterprises. Take care not to select a trading name that is already being used by another business, particularly in your industry or market sector as you may be accused of gaining benefit from their reputation (known as passing off) and this can lead to legal action being taken against you. You will also need to put your name along with the trading name of the business on your letterhead, invoices or contracts – so in this case it would read 'Mark Hall trading as Styx Enterprises'.

You do not need to register your business with anyone but you will need to personally register yourself with HM Revenue & Customs (HMRC) for Income Tax and National Insurance contributions within the first three months of trading. HMRC will send you the necessary documents to make your NIC payments and will send a Self-Assessment tax return form at the end of the financial year (end of

March) for you to complete and submit. This is easily and quickly done online now so get yourself registered to do that as well.

You should set up a bank account to keep the finances of your business separate from your personal financial matters and make sure that all income and expenditure for the business goes through this account.

Legal requirements

As a sole trader you are legally required to do the following:

- *ANNUAL TAX RETURN – You will need to make a personal annual self-assessment tax return to HMRC at the end of each financial year*

- *RECORDS – Keep thorough records showing your business income (sales including receipts from cash transactions) and expenditure (all purchases including receipts received for cash purchases) through the year and, if appropriate, VAT records including all sales and purchases made. These may be required by the tax office at any time to support what you are saying in your tax return*

Taxation

As a sole trader you will be self-employed and as such your business profits are taxed as if they are your income – you will declare this on your personal self-assessment tax return each year. You can be fined if you do not have these records available if requested to produce them. You will pay Income Tax on any profits made by the business and make fixed-rate Class 2 National Insurance contributions (these count towards things like the basic state pension, maternity allowance and bereavement benefits and are £2.40 per week for 2010/11). You will also need to make Class 4 National Insurance contributions once your profits reach a certain level – payable at 8 per cent on profits between £5,715 and £43,875 for 2010/11 plus 1 per cent on any profit over that amount.

Accounts

You will need to do annual accounts for your business. You can do these accounts for yourself if you think that you have the skills to do so and there is no standard required format laid down for them. However, we would recommend that you get an accountant to put them together for you so that you know that they are correct; they will look convincing to the tax authorities and the accountant may be able to point out things to you that may help you to optimise your tax position. A small accountancy company should charge you a few hundred pounds at the most for doing this depending upon the complexity and scale of your business and the amount of preparation work you put in. It's important to remember that the more that you do beforehand the quicker and cheaper they can produce the accounts for you. You will not be required to have your accounts audited as a sole trader.

Advantages

Easy – It's easy to start up, with limited paperwork to complete and low cost to set up. You can get started by just setting up a bank account and letting HMRC know what you are doing.

Control – You will have complete control of your business and can therefore make decisions without the requirement to get others' agreement about what you want your business to do.

Financial Rewards – You get to take all the profits of the business (providing you make a profit!).

Privacy – Because the accounts of a sole trader are not made public (unlike with a limited company) your competitors will not be able to see how your business

Disadvantages

Liability – You will have unlimited liability for any debts that the business is unable to meet. This can be a particular problem as your business grows because the level of debts tends to grow too – meaning that if the business then goes bust you will be left to pay off those debts.

Fund Raising – It can be difficult for sole traders to raise funding other than through a bank overdraft (which can be an expensive form of credit). Banks will tend not to lend anything more than quite small sums of money to small entities because of the risk involved. Where they do, it will often be on the basis that the loan is secured against the business owners' personal assets, like their house.

Advantages	Disadvantages
is performing and how you are achieving your success.	**Market Image** – Tend to look like a small company in the market place. This means that some customers will not be prepared to do business with you (because you are perceived as being unable to cope with their requirements and are a risk), staff may not want to join you (seeing you as too small scale for their career aspirations) and suppliers may be wary of supplying to you (because their fear is you may not be able to pay their bill).

2. Limited Company

What is it?

If you decide to set up your business as a limited company then, unlike the sole trader structure, your company and personal finances are kept separate from each other. Instead of you and the business being one and the same, a limited company is a completely separate entity that is owned by its *Shareholders* and managed by its *Directors*. Neither directors nor shareholders in limited liability companies are responsible for company debts, although directors may be required to personally guarantee any loans made to the business.

■ *SHAREHOLDERS – Individuals or organisations that own shares in the company. They will usually have certain rights over the decision making for the business. For example, most shareholders will have the right to vote on key decisions affecting the business and if one shareholder or a small group of shareholders holds a majority of the shares (and the rights that go with them) then they will be able to control the direction of the company. However,* at the start most companies are either formed by a single shareholder (the individual who started the business) who owns 100 per cent of the company or by two or three other shareholders alongside, with either similar or different shareholdings. The key point is that it's entirely up to you how you do this – at start-up the shares cost you nothing so you can allocate them on any basis that you like, e.g., 100 per cent to yourself, 50/50 to you and someone else, etc. But remember, typically whoever has more than 51 per cent of the shares usually has control of the decision making of the business

■ DIRECTORS – The managers of the business. As well as being responsible for ensuring that the business achieves its plans, company directors also have a number of legal, financial and administrative responsibilities. These are detailed in the Companies Act of 2006 and would cause drowsiness if we listed them here – you can find details of these responsibilities on the Companies House website and also on our site at www. whatsyourbrightidea.biz

In most smaller businesses the shareholders and directors are the same people. However, it is clearly possible to be just a shareholder and have no responsibility for the management of the business (you will find this with large companies and particularly with companies listed on stock exchanges) or just a director with no shareholding (working for the business but with no ultimate control over its direction). But we would recommend that as a business owner (shareholder) you are also a director so that you have control of your business.

Setting up

Before you can start trading as a limited company you will first need to set it up and register it with Companies House. This is known as company incorporation or formation. At first sight this can look complicated but these days setting up a company is simple, if you know what you are doing. Traditionally you would need to go to an accountant or agent and ask them to do this for you (and you still can) but now it's simple to do this online by going to one of many company incorporation websites.

Your limited company will need to have a name that is not being used by any other business in your market, industry or sector – clearly you may need to be a little creative around this because with over 5 million businesses in the UK quite a lot of names are already taken. As the owner of the business you will almost certainly be the main (or even sole) shareholder and a director of the company. A limited company needs to have one director and must have a company secretary – nowadays one person can do these two roles.

The online incorporation company will probably offer a number of different packages (the basic package usually has everything that you need) for between £40 and £90. A basic package will include:

- *Company name check – to tell you if the name that you want to use for your business is available*

- *Preparation and filing with Companies House on your behalf of the company formation documents. These are:*

  1. *Memorandum of Association – includes company name, address and type of business*

  2. *Articles of Association – includes details of the directors' powers and shareholder rights*

  3. *Form IN01 – details of the company's registered office, details of the Company Secretary and Director(s) and details of the shareholders*

- *Bank account introduction – if you do not have a bank account they often have special offers such as an initial free banking period*

- *Companies House £15 registration fee*

Once you have completed the online application you will be sent copies of the key documents either in the post or simply as electronic copies by email. The incorporation company will register your company with Companies House – the government body that is responsible for company registration in the UK. This registration must be complete before you can start trading although you are under no obligation to start trading once you have your registration – you can delay this until you are ready. If you need to get started in a hurry you can apply for a same-day service or even buy an existing company that is already incorporated, but not trading, 'off the shelf'.

If you have any concerns about this process, it is usually best to approach an accountant to do it on your behalf. They will charge you a small fee to do the company incorporation but this can be worth it to ensure that there are no problems and that you get it right.

Legal requirements

All limited companies are required to do the following:

- *ANNUAL COMPANIES HOUSE RETURN –* Submit an annual return to Companies House each year – this simply updates basic information about your company and takes about five minutes to complete online at www.companieshouse.gov.uk. Companies House will send you a reminder and there is a filing fee of £15

- *ANNUAL ACCOUNTS –* Submit a set of annual accounts to HMRC. You will almost certainly need an accountant to do this for you, unless you are suitably qualified to do it yourself

- *ANNUAL HMRC CORPORATION TAX RETURN –* This informs HMRC if your company has made any profits in the year. You will need to complete a form CT600 that shows this, along with a spreadsheet showing how you made your Corporation Tax calculation. Once submitted, HMRC will tell you how much your Corporation

Tax bill will be (for 2010 this is 21 per cent on profits up to £300,000). Any Corporation Tax that is due must be paid to HMRC within nine months of the company year-end each year or you will be fined and charged interest on the late payment

■ *MONTHLY PAYE AND NIC RETURN – If you employ staff. Anyone employed by the company must pay Income Tax and National Insurance on their income. Also the company must pay National Insurance on its employees. It is the company's responsibility to calculate the amount of taxation and NICs for each employee and pay this to HMRC*

In all of the legal requirements shown above, you are advised to get your accountant to ensure that it is done correctly.

Accounts

As a limited company you will be required to submit accounts in a format laid down by law and must adhere to a set of accounting standards, many of which are beyond the knowledge of most small business owners. Accounts must be submitted once a year for small businesses. Getting an accountant to do this for your business is essential – they will make sure that you stick to the guidelines, advise of changes to the rules and regulations and ensure that your accounts are submitted to the right place on your behalf. Depending upon the amount and complexity of the work involved, a simple small business should be able to do this for between £400 and £1,000 each year.

In order to help put these accounts together and to act as evidence that what you have submitted is correct, the company will need to keep the following records throughout the year:

■ *TRADING RECORDS – Including bank statements, paying-in books, purchase invoices, business expenses and sales receipts*

- *VAT RECORDS* – If you are registered for VAT, all VAT sales and purchase invoices and import and export documentation if appropriate

- *PAYROLL RECORDS* – If you have staff, details of gross pay, tax, employers and employees NI and net pay

Advantages

Limited Liability – If things go wrong and a limited company fails, its directors and share-holders have 'limited liability' in that their personal assets cannot be touched.

Market Image – May look more 'professional', it may help if you need to raise external finance, and it may be more tax efficient than other business structures.

Company Name – By registering your company you will protect its name so that no one else can use it.

Raising Funds – You can bring in new shareholders by selling them some of the company's shares in return for their cash, quickly and easily.

Employee Participation – You can offer shares or share options in the company to your employees. This can help to motivate and reward them.

Disadvantages

Directors' Responsibilities – Limited company directors have more responsibilities than sole traders and these need to be taken very seriously as failure to comply with them can lead to directors being declared 'unfit' and dis-qualified from being a director again for up to 15 years. However, by understanding what the rules are and using a bit of common sense this does not usually pre-sent difficulties for any but a few.

More Administration – Running a limited company involves the completion of more paperwork and dealing with more govern-ment organisations than for a sole trader or a partnership.

Accounting Requirements – These are clearly more onerous and complicated than for sole traders or partnerships as you are required to adhere to an obligatory accounting format and rules.

Advantages

Taxation - Companies pay Corporation Tax on their profits - the level of Corporation Tax tends to be lower than the rate of Income Tax.

Continuity - As a distinct legal entity, the company will continue even if you should resign or die - if you are looking to be able to pass something on this can be important and not the case if you set up as a sole trader.

3. Partnership

What is it?

A partnership is a type of business structure in which two or more people (large partnerships may have thousands of partners) share the responsibilities, costs, rewards and risks of being in business together. A partnership offers a simpler way to get started than a limited company and is similar in many ways to how an individual would set up and run in the sole trader structure. The partners own the business and take a share - usually, though not always, in equal proportion - of the profits or losses made by the business. They may also have 'sleeping' partners who might put money into your business but are not involved in the day-to-day management. This is often a structure used by professional services businesses, like accountants, lawyers and management consultancies and sometimes by husband and wife teams.

As with sole traders, partners are self-employed rather than being employed by the business. A partnership can employ other people but unless they too are made partners they will not own any of the business. Partners are personally liable for any debts that the partnership may generate and do not have their liability to them protected in the way that they would if they were in a limited company. So creditors can claim a partner's personal assets to pay their debts. Also if you are going to use this structure be aware that your assets could be used to pay off your share of the partnership's debts even if the debt was created by another partner.

Limited Liability Partnerships (LLPs)

In order to allow some protection to business owners operating within this structure, Limited Liability Partnerships (LLPs) have become more common. These are similar to the general partnerships described above, but the LLP itself is responsible for any debts that it accumulates rather than the individual partners.

Setting up

For a general partnership, this is very straightforward. As with the sole trader structure, a partnership has no separate legal existence from the individual partners and there are no legal requirements to set up or incorporate a partnership or register it with Companies House. However, if you choose this structure, you should definitely put in place a formal written contract to cover the aims of the business and how you intend to run it – how much capital is being put in and by whom; individuals' roles and responsibilities; who owns what assets, how the profits will be divided; what happens if someone leaves; and so on. Business partnerships are very much like personal relationships – things can change over a long period of time and in our experience there is much 'falling out' with this type of business structure – so rather like a pre-nuptial agreement, put in place a partnership agreement (called a deed of partnership) for the divorce rather than the marriage, just in case. A solicitor is the best person to go for help with this.

If you are setting up an LLP you will need to submit an Incorporation Document (Form LLP2) to Companies House to advise them of your LLP's name, registered office, partners' names and which partners are designated to carry out the legal requirements of the partnership, such as signing the accounts and making the annual return to Companies House.

Legal requirements

As a partnership you are legally required to do the following:

- *HMRC REGISTRATION* – Each partner will need to initially register personally as self-employed with HMRC and advise them that they are starting a business, as described for Sole Traders above

- *ANNUAL PARTNERSHIP TAX RETURN* – The partnership will need to submit an annual tax return to HMRC and will pay Income Tax and make NICs on all profits made

- *ANNUAL PERSONAL TAX RETURN* – Each individual partner will also need to make their own annual personal self-assessment tax return to HMRC. Each of the partners' business income is counted alongside any other personal income

- *RECORD KEEPING* – Partnerships will need to keep good records of all trading activities as described in the Sole Trader section above

Accounts

As with the sole trader structure, your annual accounts as a partnership do not need to comply with a legally enforced structure, but they will still need to be done according to the standard and accepted accounting practice. So getting an accountant is the sensible approach for most partnerships. LLPs are also treated more like a sole trader than a limited company when it comes to accounting and taxation. As with Sole Traders, partners in an LLP pay the flat rate Class 2 National Insurance contributions (NICs) in the same way as self-employed people, and income tax and Class 4 NICs on their share of the partnership profits. Although only one partner needs to return the partnership return, both partners are equally liable to pay income tax.

Advantages

Sharing – As a partner you will share the financial risks and rewards with your other partners and pool your different strengths, skills and experience for the good of the business.

Flexibility – The distribution of profits is much more flexible in a general partnership than they are in limited companies (where dividends are usually distributed according to the amount of shares held). Because of this, an individual partner can be rewarded with a higher share of the profits if they have contributed more to the business regardless of their shareholding.

Easy Set-up – General partnerships can be started quickly and without the need to register them. You can start trading when you like.

Low Administration – There are few registration or reporting requirements.

Disadvantages

Differences of Opinion – Partners may have different visions or goals for the business, unequal commitment in terms of time and finances and there could be (and often are) personal disagreements.

Liabilities – Partners are 'jointly' liable with each other for all of the debts that the business may have. So if the business should fail and one partner does not or cannot pay their share, you will still be required to pay even if you had no responsibility for the obligation or did not know that it was there. Insurance policies to mitigate this occurrence are a good idea when setting up an LLP.

Fund Raising – It can be difficult for partnerships to raise large amounts of funding even though they can in theory sell a proportion of their equity to new partners; typically there are a limited number of sellers of this equity and the personal liability for the new partner can be off-putting.

Continuity – If one of the partners resigns, dies or goes bankrupt, the partnership must be dissolved.

Making the Decision

Accountants and other professional advisers continue to have debates about the relative merits and demerits of limited companies, partnerships and being a sole trader.

The reasons for being a sole trader are often a balance between business and personal costs and benefits. While it is the simplest, quickest and easiest vehicle to administer, it carries the risks associated with unlimited liability and you will always look small in the market place. Often, this risk makes potential business owners opt for some other type of business structure particularly as their business becomes more successful and the accompanying risks tend to grow too. At this point you have the option of forming a limited liability company.

Partnerships offer a quick and easy way for two or more people to pursue their common objective and to complement each other with skills, knowledge and capital – a pooling of resources. But over time there are often problems with disagreements about direction and perceptions that one is doing more work/adding more value than another. Having a strong deed of partnership is essential (even if you think that you get on really well with each other now) and setting up an LLP can reduce your personal risk.

While in some cases there may be tax advantages to partnerships over limited companies, the latter offers just about all of the benefits of a partnership but without the liabilities that go with it. Limited companies allow new funding to be introduced relatively easily; shares can be offered to attract and reward staff, and this structure can often look more convincing to customers. The price that you pay for all this is that it's more complicated and expensive to administer, but actually not vastly so once you get the hang of it.

Overall our advice is to start off either as a sole trader and then be ready to move to a limited company as you grow or go straight to a limited company structure. When you are working through all the issues concerning setting up and the legal and governmental requirements, do get professional advice, especially from an accountant. Consider the relative advantages and disadvantages of the main types of business structure and don't be afraid to change if you think that a different way would be beneficial. In particular, consider the optimal tax position by discussing with an accountant how much you think you are going to generate in sales, what expenditure you will make and how much you intend to earn yourself. Having a well-put together cash flow forecast can help with this analysis.

Bank Account

Whatever structure you decide upon, you will need a business bank account. This is the centre of your financial affairs. It's ring-fenced from your personal affairs. Think of it as a big wall between you and it – there are some rules and regulations about what you can and cannot do with it, particularly when you are operating as a limited company or partnership. Breaking these can lead you into fraudulent activities that you will definitely want to avoid.

Value Added Tax (VAT)

You will need to decide if you should register for VAT whether you are a sole trader, limited company or a partnership if you are going to make sales of £70,000 (2010/11 figure) or more per year. Remember what we said earlier – if you are charging VAT, not everything you make in sales income is your money. Simply put, you are a tax collector for the government. You don't need to register too early for VAT as you can do this when you think that your annual turnover is going to break through the threshold. If you keep regular management accounts, you will be able to easily see when the time has come to register. Don't get overexcited about the prospects of being able to claim back VAT on expenses. Whilst this may look attractive – an opportunity to get something back – it's not always such a good idea. Weigh up the benefits of making reclaims on what you spend against the increase that you will be charging your customers for your product or service.

Paying Yourself

At some point you'll probably be looking to earn some income from your business. In fact we would argue that this is essential – at

Bright Ideas Trust we never support a business owner who is not paying themselves. You'll find that even hard-nosed venture capitalists don't like managements that don't earn a living because you need to keep healthy and be focused on running the business, not worrying about money. But by the same token, you should not be thinking about getting rich just yet – in the early stages it's important to keep cash in the business to support its growth. When you are thinking about paying yourself, work out what your bare minimum to survive on is (rent, mortgage, food, utility bills) and if you can't pay yourself that much then think hard about doing this. Otherwise you will not be able to do it anyway because you will be so down or ill. Think of it as your travel survival kit – the bare minimum you can get by on. The way in which you can pay yourself varies depending upon the business vehicle that you have.

How do you pay yourself? This often trips people up. They start running their business; they generate sales and get income. Their business bank account starts to swell with cash. They think, that's good, I'm doing well here; I'll take the money I've made for myself. Often it's burned a hole in their pocket before they've had a chance to select the next horse at Newmarket or book a cruise. But the key point to remember is that the money in the business bank account is not yours. It belongs to the business. And the business will in effect need to agree to you as an individual taking its money out in salary, drawings or dividends. The way that you can do this varies by business structure:

- *LIMITED COMPANIES – Pay yourself a wage or salary or take a share of the profits at the end of the year – known as dividends – or a mixture of these two*

- *SOLE TRADERS – 'Drawings' – usually a small monthly wage based on the minimum amount on which you need to live*

- *PARTNERSHIPS – Pay yourself a wage or salary and/or take a share of the business's profits as dividends at the end of the year*

GETTING READY FOR DEPARTURE

FUNDING

'There's no such thing as a free lunch.' Anon

In this chapter we will look at different types and sources of funding that are available to you as a start-up business owner. We discuss the circumstances in which you should consider funding and provide guidance on how to be successful at raising money from these sources.

Why Funding?

Most new businesses will need some initial funding to get them going. This is money that you will be investing into your business to buy raw materials, equipment, rent an office, do some marketing or pay your living expenses while you're getting ready to win your first customers and generate income from them. Clearly you want to get a customer to buy something from you as quickly as possible because in effect this is the best funding you can get. But this does not usually happen on day one, so in the meantime you may need some start-up (or 'seed') capital. You will have a Business Plan that shows that you will start to make a profit – and equally importantly a positive cashflow – at a point in the future, but you need to put things in place before you can get to that point. This is the funding gap – the period before you start generating income from customers but where you will need to spend some money to allow you to do that – so you will need to finance this.

Do I Need Funding?

It's not a guess or based on a feeling. As we have seen, your Financial Forecast, and in particular a Cashflow Forecast, will tell you whether or not you need to raise funds and how much money you think you will need to reach the point where income from customers is sufficient to make your business viable. It will not only tell you how much you need to bridge the gap, but also which week or month you need it, what the total amount required to bridge the gap is, when you will be able to pay it back and what impact the repayments will then make on your financial position.

What Type of Funding?

There are essentially two main types of funding open to you.

Debt

This is where another person or organisation will lend you money in return for the repayment of the sum that they lent plus the payment of interest on top. Usually payments are spread equally over a period of time, for example, one to three years, although sometimes the loan may be repayable as one lump sum at the end of a period of time. Most of us are familiar with debt financing – it's the way that personal bank loans and mortgages work and is straightforward to get your head around. The loan consists of two parts – the Principal sum (the amount that you are borrowing, say £5,000) and the Interest sum (the total amount of interest that you will need to pay back to the lender for the privilege of using their money). For example, if you borrow £10,000 at an interest rate of 10 per cent with the interest all added at the end of the year then the interest sum will be £1,000. Interest is typically added to the regular repayment so that you make, for example, 24 or 36 equal repayments that will be made up of the Principal plus Interest. Your Cashflow Forecast will need to reflect the fact that a loan repayment will go out regularly, probably once a month on the same day each month, to the lender. If you only require a relatively small amount of funding for a short time you could consider a simple overdraft on your bank account to bridge the gap, although interest rates on these can be relatively high.

Equity

This is where another person or organisation invests their money in return for a share in your business. In order to do this you will need to be set up as a limited company, so that you can sell them some of the shares of that company, or as a partnership. You will not be required to pay back any of their money, which can be very advantageous particularly while you are growing your business and will want to conserve all the cash that you can rather than paying it out as loan repayments. But the investor will own some of your business and as a result will usually have the right to a share in the profits that you make (paid as dividends) and will take their share of anything that you make if you sell your business to someone else in the future. The investor will usually also have certain rights over the decision making of the company in line with the amount of shares or equity that they own. Typically, those that make equity investments will be looking for you to sell your business at some stage so that they can make their return on their investment in this way. So bear in mind that they may want decisions about the company's future to reflect this desire – and some of the decisions may not match your preferred route!

But there is a third approach that we recommend you consider.

'Bootstrapping'

The term 'bootstrapping' comes from the idea that you lift yourself up from the ground by the straps of your boots without external help. Applied to business this means that you will aim to finance the initial stages of your business out of your own pocket for just long enough to get the first revenues from customers and then to use these revenues to fund the next period of your development. And so little by little you pull yourself up by carefully managing the incoming revenues from customers, spending just enough to grow a bit bigger and maybe saving some for a later day. This approach means that you need to be very careful with your expenditure and work hard to make the most of your limited resources, always trying to do things as cost effectively as possible and concentrating hard on keeping your costs under control. Taking this road usually means that you will not be able to grow your business quickly because you will not be able to invest much in the things needed to achieve growth quickly, at least not until you can save and build up cash in your bank account.

Many would argue that the disciplines required to take a bootstrapping approach to building a business should apply to any business because getting the most out of every penny that you spend should be the aim whether you are a greengrocer on the Chiswick High Road or managing a FTSE 100 company. Sadly, it is not always like that and many well-funded businesses spend much too freely believing that the font of cash is bottomless. To paraphrase Warren Buffett, the legendary business financier, 'If you're smart you don't need to borrow money, and if you're not smart then you have no business borrowing anyway.' And this would therefore seem to support the bootstrapping and good management discipline approach.

There is no right and wrong about which way you go to get funding. Any of these approaches is acceptable when looking for finance for your business. Clearly, they have advantages and disadvantages and we'll come on to those when we look at the different sources of funding below. But before you knee-jerk into trying to raise funding, think hard about whether you really do need it, how much you need and what strings you would consider accepting as part of the deal that you will make to get it. Then if you do need it take a look at the options open to you and decide what's right for your situation.

Where to Look for Funding

Where you look will be largely determined by how much funding you are seeking, the type of funding, at what stage of development your business is and whether or not you want other sorts of help from your funder along with the money.

There are many different sources of finance for new businesses. Different stages require different sources. Your chances of securing money from one or more of them will be hugely improved if you have followed the steps outlined in this book – a well thought-through Business Proposition with a Business Plan and a robust set of Financial Forecasts will all be required to persuade experienced investors and lenders that you are a suitable place for their cash.

In the course of our work at Bright Ideas Trust, we are often asked about where new businesses can go in search of finance. The answer to that question usually starts with another question: 'How much do you need?' How much you need is, by this stage, not guesswork – your Business Plan and Financial Forecast will tell you this. As a rough rule of thumb you can use the following to point you in the right direction.

Me, myself and I

First of all, can you find the money that you need from your own means? This is a good starting point because you will not be required to give up anything to someone else and will keep control of your own destiny. So starting from that position, try to finance it yourself first. This is usually not only the smart option but an essential one – even if you raise funds from others, it's important that you do put some of your own money into your venture – think how it would look if you went to ask others for money and had to tell them that you were not investing yourself. Always remember that starting your own business is a type of gamble, not like a bet on the horses or roulette wheel, but a gamble nonetheless. As with any type of bet, don't risk more than you can afford to lose of your own money. Typically, finding the funds for yourself is most appropriate where relatively small amounts are required – if you need more you will probably be looking to others to get involved. So if you cannot fund things for yourself where do you go next?

Ask the family

The next port of call can be your family and/or friends. Again, this is not often a source of large amounts of funding but can be a good way to get you started. Friends and family will usually support you financially without imposing onerous terms on you in return for their cash, e.g., high rates of interest, wanting a stake in your business. While this might seem like an informal and relaxed way of gaining access to finance, you should still put in place some sort of formal agreement with them. This can be as simple as a letter setting out the main terms of your agreement (how much is being lent, what the repayment will be) and signed by both of you. It's best to get an accountant or a solicitor to draw something up if you want to do this properly. If you choose this path, bear in mind that should things go wrong and your friends and family lose their money this can lead to difficulties. So make it clear from the outset that they are taking a risk to help you and that while this may reward them they may also lose.

Your family and friends will probably not need to see a detailed plan and so if you are intending to pursue this approach you may be inclined to think that this will let you off doing one. But don't use this as an excuse not to do one.

Banks

Banks have traditionally been an early destination for anyone looking to raise finance to start a business. The recent economic turmoil has led to a much greater reluctance by the banks to make loans to small businesses, which has meant that it's become increasingly difficult to raise investment capital just at the time when it's most needed to help foster one of the key ways back to economic growth. But this does not mean that you should give up on this avenue; funding for a good business case can still be obtained and, as we emerge from recession, access to bank finance will improve. Generally there are two main types of finance available from banks: overdrafts and loans.

- OVERDRAFTS – This is most suitable when you have a short-term requirement for a relatively small amount of money. Typically an overdraft is easy to obtain once you have an account with a particular bank and, once agreed, gives you immediate access to funds without the need to go and ask again. The bank will agree a maximum amount that you can overdraw on your account and an interest rate applicable on the amount that you take. The interest rate will typically be a few percentage points above the prevailing Bank of England (BoE) Base Rate and is usually added monthly. Always make sure that you agree the overdraft rather than just go overdrawn without telling the bank, as the latter will cost you considerably more. Either way, it is not recommended that your business should stay indebted in this way for long. You must find a less expensive way if you need funds over the medium to longer term

- LOANS – This is a better solution if you require larger sums of money to invest in your business. Loans can be arranged to fit with your specific needs so that amount, duration and interest rate can all be flexed to suit your requirements. You should consider the following components if you are thinking about going down this path:

    - AMOUNT – Can be anything from a few hundred pounds to several hundred thousand pounds

    - INTEREST RATE – Can be fixed or variable; usually based on being a few percentage points above the BoE Base Rate

- ■ *DURATION – Can be anything between a few months (usually not less than twelve) and twenty or thirty years in a few cases*

- ■ *BREAKS AND HOLIDAYS – There may be opportunities to stop paying the capital sum and only pay interest for a period, or take a complete payment 'holiday' (make no payments at all) for a time, or some other flexing of your loan*

A loan gives you clear visibility of what you are getting yourself into – showing you the monthly repayment amount and how many months you will be paying back for. This means that you have good information on which to plan your business (such as your cashflow forecast) and no nasty surprises when you open your bank statement at the end of the month.

If you want to get a bank loan, banks will want to see a well-presented Business Plan. They will not be prepared to take much of a risk (unlike a business angel or venture capital company) and so will be looking for investment opportunities that have been well thought through, managed by individuals who look like they know what they are doing and where they think that they have a good chance of getting their money back. They will usually require you to make some sort of guarantee that may include securing other assets that you own personally against the debt – if you fail to pay back they may want to reclaim their loan in this way.

Business angels

If you're looking for larger amounts of funding, between say £25,000 and £250,000, then you will probably be out of the sphere of normal bank lending. At the same time, you will be below the minimum threshold that a venture capital company would consider – often a minimum of about £1m – plus you will be at too early and risky a stage for them to consider you as a suitable investment opportunity. Business angels tend to bridge the gap between friends and family/ banks and the venture capital companies.

Angels are individuals who are wealthy enough to have funds available to make investments in early stage businesses in return for a share of that business. Typically, they are looking to build up a portfolio of business investments, often but not always in a particular industry sector where they have experience and knowledge. They will usually be interested in your business not just for financial reasons and will want to meet several times to get a good understanding of your business plan before concluding an investment. If you are going to attract them to invest in your business then you will need to be able to show how they will gain a return on their investment of several times what they originally put in – anything between four and ten times their investment. So they are usually only appropriate if you are planning an equity or exit-driven business.

Often business angels invest not just for financial reasons. Many are retired or semi-retired and get involved with start-up and early stage companies so that they can keep up to date with what's happening in a particular industry and can pass on their knowledge as well as their money to the next generation of business owners. Because of this they offer you much more than just their money: their valuable network of contacts can connect you with potential customers, partners, suppliers and other useful people and organisations. They can also be a source of finding mentors.

It is estimated that there are somewhere between 15,000 and 20,000 angels in the UK. Many have organised themselves into groups who look at investment opportunities and invest together. You can find these by looking at the British Business Angels Association website. In summary, angels will evaluate an investment proposition on the basis of the business plan, the expertise and track record of the management, competitive edge or unique selling points, growth potential in your market, the personal skills of and compatibility between the management and the financial commitment of the business owner.

Government money

Alongside all of these funding sources, you have the opportunity to apply for the wide range of financing schemes available these days from central and local government, regional development agencies and the European Union. You can find up-to-date details of many of the current sources of government money on our website (www. whatsyourbrightidea.biz). When considering this avenue bear in mind the following points:

■ *USUALLY FREE* – Obviously the single most important attraction. Usually these schemes offer you finance at no cost (grants, allowances and awards) or, at worst, very low cost (inexpensive loans)

■ *SPECIFIC* – These schemes tend to offer funding for a particular industry, business size, business location or the type of demographic group that the owner or employees come from, such as women, young people, older people, disabled, ethnic groups and so on. Also, they will often only be available where your business is going to use the money for a specific purpose (e.g., research and development) of if you will create jobs in an area

■ *COMPLICATED* – With thousands of schemes out there, it is doubtful that any one person in the world knows all about all of them, and they tend to be introduced and withdrawn frequently. Just finding your way to the right scheme for your circumstances can take time and determination

■ *TIME CONSUMING* – Applying for these types of schemes usually involves putting together detailed proposals or plans or filling out lengthy application forms

■ *COMPETITIVE* – The opportunity to get access to 'free money' is as appealing to the next business owner as it might be to you. There are only limited resources available, even though there are lots of schemes, so be prepared to have to compete for it

■ *MATCHING* – In many cases you will be required to find other sources of funds to go *alongside the government money in order to secure it. This is known as 'matched funding'*

Business support organisations

As well as government there are a number of non-governmental business support organisations that offer advice, guidance and funding for start-up and early stage businesses. Typically, these organisations are set up as charities and can offer finance in the form of grants and loans alongside the all-important mentoring and professional services support, such as accountancy and finance, which you may need to help you get started. This support is generally free of charge. You can find an up-to-date list of these organisations on our website at www.whatsyourbrightidea.biz.

Summary – No Free Lunch

If you do ultimately go to external sources of funding there is usually a price to pay, unless you have a sugar daddy who is willing to fund you for nothing – but there are not that many Roman Abramovichs in the world . . . Banks will want interest on a loan, while equity investors, like business angels and venture capital companies, will want a share of your business and maybe even some control over decision making. Some financial institutions will want you to give personal guarantees, often in the form of putting your house or some other personal asset on the line, so that in the event that your business cannot meet its commitments to them, you will be personally on the hook. Balance the risks with the reward, think about your own personal appetite for risk, discuss it with your mentor, and go into funding with your eyes open and some good guidance. Mistakes here can be costly, both financially and emotionally, and difficult to correct later. But getting funding can also hold the key to the door of your success.

Just about every successful business owner that we know will advise you to do as much funding as you can for yourself without going to others for it. At the same time, if you really cannot get going without the need for external funding then definitely take it even if it costs you a relatively high amount to get it. Negotiate hard on how much you pay or give up to secure the funds but, in the end, remember that it's better to own 50 per cent of a lot than 100 per cent of nothing. Don't be frightened of giving up some of your business to others who have the skills, expertise and contacts that will complement you if you believe that they can help you to build your business into something bigger.

Bear in mind that your potential investor or funder is interested in, first, getting their money back and, second, making a return on that money. Some will also offer you advice and guidance, but more are driven by their own desire to keep some control on their investment by being involved in the decision making rather than any philanthropic outlook.

Most importantly, ensure that you have enough funds to get your business going to the point where your customers will be providing you with income from things that you have sold to them, to finance your company and give you a profit. You want to get the right amount – not too little so that you cannot function properly, but equally not too much so that the funds are sitting idle and not working for you (or the provider of the funds).

Top ten funding pointers

1 **Up Your Aspirations** – Try to raise more than you think that you need – get the right amount but have some contingency because things usually cost more than expected and income builds slower than you think. Asking a second time is not impossible but is more difficult. You may need to adjust your business plan and financial forecasts to show how this greater amount would work to a lender or investor

2 **Skin in the Game** – You should always invest financially in your own business. External investors will usually ask you what skin you have in the game and you will need to be able to show them that you are committed with both your time and your money

3 **Right Place, Right Time** – Think carefully about whether or not you need funding in the first place. Do as much of it for yourself as you can afford before going to external funders, then have a clear plan of what type of funding you want, how much and what you can afford to give up for it

4   **Wow Factor** – Make sure that you prepare and make a strong presentation to potential investors or lenders. They are right when they say that 'you will never get a second chance to make a good first impression' and typically you will only get one hour with an investor, so make sure you make the most of it

5   **Outnumbered** – Know your numbers off by heart. Make sure that they are well researched and clearly presented. Investors will examine these in detail and if you are not prepared and cannot answer their questions quickly and accurately you will raise fear and uncertainty in their minds

6   **I'm So Excited!** – Make it exciting – show them that you are going to put your all into making this work and what's in it for them as well as you. If you are presenting to equity investors, leave them drooling over how much money you are going to make for them

7   **Be Persistent** – Most people who have tried to raise money will tell you that being rejected by those that you approach for funds is the most common response. You will need all of your passion and commitment to keep trying in the face of this

8   **Security** – If you're looking for debt finance, you may be asked to put your personal assets up as a guarantee against not being able to repay the loan. Securing loans on your house or giving personal guarantees is a serious undertaking; so do not take it lightly or without ensuring that others in your life who might be affected by it know what you're doing

9   **Pitch It** – When you do get to present to investors, be punctual (actually a few minutes early), well turned out and polite. Try to be confident and assured in what you are doing without being arrogant. Make sure you tell them what you are looking for from them

10 **Right Type** – Choose your source of investment or funding based on the amount you need, your stage of development and what additional support you might want from them. Be sure to ask them to tell you how they will help you as well as providing finance

CREATING MOMENTUM

'Remember what Bilbo used to say: It's a dangerous business, Frodo, going out your door. You step onto the road, and if you don't keep your feet, there's no knowing where you might be swept off to.' J. R. R. Tolkien

While you are putting in place the funding you require and refining your Business Plan, there are a number of practical things you can get on with to enable you to hit the ground running when you formally launch your business. These momentum-creating activities will also help you to better prepare and plan as you go along.

Get On With It

By now you've probably had just about enough of thinking, planning and writing and just want to get on with it. There is much that you can, and should, be getting on with while you're doing your thinking, planning and writing. So don't be afraid to crack on with some of it. Unlike the risk-averse Hobbit quoted above, don't be frightened to take a walk outside and risk being swept away, or at least along. And don't let anyone tell you that you must have everything fully worked out before you start doing anything. Creating a brilliant and elegant Business Proposition and Business Plan in the proverbial ivory tower is just as bad as rushing out there without thinking it through properly. We've seen many elegant Business Plans compiled with little real-world practicality that have gone on to fail because they hadn't taken some of the baby steps required ahead of launching.

Experience shows that there is a balance to be found between *thinking it through* and *getting on with it*. Some people just like to set off; others like to plan in minute detail first. Both approaches are acceptable providing you are not right at either end of the spectrum. All businesses need some planning so you can't just ignore it. Similarly, you do need to get on with some things while you're planning – it's just about getting the balance right.

The Big 'Mo'

It's important that you start to create this momentum, or what is sometimes called 'market traction', while you're thinking through your plans. But you may ask: 'How can I possibly start doing things when I'm not sure that I know what I'm doing?' Sometimes you will need to use a bit of audacity and do things even though you know that you don't know what you're doing.

As is now well recognised, by doing things – and making some mistakes, looking slightly foolish or possibly even a bit unprofessional – you will learn more about how to put your plans together and make your proposition and plan better for it. 'Learning by doing' is one of the best ways of learning – learning the hard way in the school of hard knocks. This is how we get the precious experience that is so valuable in business as in life. Don't be afraid of making some mistakes; it's more important to give it a go and sometimes fail than to sit on your hands and die wondering.

So what can you get on with while you're working out how your business is going to work? There are many things that you can do to create momentum. We call this the 'Big Mo'. Here are some tried and tested ways to create market momentum or traction so that when you're ready to launch you will hit the ground running. We call it the 'Ten P List'.

1 **Practice** – Rehearse your sales pitch

2 **Presentation** – Get one together

3 **Prove it** – Create a visualisation, demonstration or prototype

4 **Prime yourself** – Train for it

5 **Pilot scheme** – Test the market

6 **Participate** – Get work experience

7 **Press the flesh** – Network

8 **Prospect** – Build your sales pipeline

9 **Pry** – Check out your competition

10 **Personal life** – Get ready for a change of life

1. Practice

We'll spend more time later talking about sales and selling but at this stage take it that you can get started in some way. Sales is the most important thing that you can do when you have your own business.

Selling is often a word that can strike fear into the hearts of a would-be business owner. This is not surprising since many people have little or no experience of doing it, and are therefore sometimes afraid of the unknown. Also, given our human instinct to take rejection rather badly (there will be some of that unfortunately), we may tend to shy away from it. But just about everything that you will do when you have your own business will have some impact upon, and be geared towards, making sales.

But before you get to the stage where you are ready to try to win customers, you can try something else out first. Think of it as a sort of pre-sales activity. Identify one or two individuals or companies that you think might ultimately be prospects for what you are going to be offering and ask them for their advice. If you are asking for advice rather than for a meeting at which you are trying to sell them something, most people will readily agree, providing they have the time. Once you're there, do your sales pitch, present what you are intending to do and ask for their feedback. Listen carefully to what they tell you, and you will learn huge amounts about their view of what you are offering, your pricing, how it stacks up against the competition (who they are probably buying from already), what's important to them as customers, what they like and don't like, and so on.

By doing this you can practise your sales pitch with the advantage of a safety net – if you make mistakes it doesn't matter – and you get valuable feedback to either confirm that you are on the right lines or to help you to improve things. Consider doing this many times and when you get into operation take the opportunity to do as many sales meetings and presentations as you can. Practice makes you perfect, rather like a well-honed golf swing, which requires thousands of repetitions to achieve perfection.

2. Presentation

Put together an initial version of a slide presentation about your business. You can use it not only with potential customers but at any time to talk about your business – this could be to the bank, an investor, a supplier, when recruiting staff or to the press. So even if you are intending to open a retail store or set up a web-based business, or can't see a time when you'll ever need to make a presentation to customers, it's a good thing to have.

As recipients of hundreds of PowerPoint presentations, we know that many people dread having to sit through this type of presentation; there is not much worse than seeing someone sit opposite you with a thick deck of slides and announce that they will just give you a brief presentation of their business plan. We wonder what the full-length version might look like! However, don't be deterred – it remains the most common and acceptable way to present information to others about your business and, providing you keep it brief and to the point, most people will actually appreciate this method of delivery. So put together a short PowerPoint slide presentation (between five and fifteen pages in length) and improve and refine it each time you present it to someone. When you are starting out it's very helpful to have your sales story on a few slides so that you make sure you cover everything and have a crib sheet to get back on track if you get lost or go wrong. Once you're well practised you can dispense with it.

You will already have created some of what it should contain as you put together your Business Proposition. It should cover the following areas and you should be able to get everything you need on to a maximum of ten slides:

- *Who we are*
- *What we do*
- *What we can do for you*
- *Why we are good/different*
- *Endorsements*
- *What we are asking for*
- *Contact details*

3. Prove it

It's what the great Dale Carnegie in his classic book called *How to Win Friends and Influence People* described as 'Dramatising Things'. Bring your product or service to life by creating a mock-up, prototype, demonstration or visualisation. When Fabien Souzandry came to see us about funding for v.ographics, his nascent film production business, he brought along his showreel of many of the films that he had created. This was very powerful as it showed us what he was asking us to invest in. Similarly, Nike Akinola, a young fashion designer, had illustrations of her next collection and samples of garments already made. If you are intending to create an Internet-based business, produce some mock-ups of what the website will look like. If you're producing a product, try to get a prototype or at least professional-standard technical drawings.

Always carry these things around with you. You never know when you will get the chance to pitch to a potential customer, partner or investor and this will help you to bring it to life. People like to touch and feel things to help them understand what you are talking about. Some people have a much greater ability to understand through visual things, some through listening, some by playing/ interacting with a prototype. So cover all the bases. And always 'eat your own dog food' – prove that you have confidence in your own product or service by using it. So if you make clothes or jewellery or fashion accessories or swimwear then make sure you wear them when you can.

4. Prime yourself

Get yourself some training in the skills required for your business. While Sean Brown was setting up his commercial cleaning business he went on a six-week industrial cleaning course to learn how to do the job properly and to gain an accreditation while he was at it. Not only did this give him many useful tools and techniques to help improve what he could offer to his customers, it gave him a stronger sales story with potential customers, authority when managing his cleaning staff and greater self-confidence from knowing that he was doing it right.

5. Pilot scheme

Once you have done some thinking about what your product or service is and shared this with others to get their feedback, then you can create a Proof of Concept. This is an initial limited version of your product or service that can demonstrate and prove that it works and that customers are interested in buying from you. For example, if you plan to make things, whether it be clothes or jam or children's toys, make some initial samples of your product. You can then devise a test trading campaign through which you aim to demonstrate that there is a market for your product or service by selling what you have to offer on a small and manageable scale.

We've worked with a number of people who have hired a small market stall or space in a shopping mall for a weekend for this purpose. We also worked with Kofi and Nana, two guys who set up Ballerz League, a business running an inner city six-a-side football league – a service business. Before we helped them with investment and mentoring support they had already run a trial league with just a few teams to see if there was a market with real needs, if they could sell to that market and how it might work out when they delivered the service to their customers. Fortunately for them they found that it did all work but they learned many things along the way and, more importantly, were able to show us real evidence that it could be done. We backed them.

6. Participate
Go and get some work experience in your chosen industry or market. Work for someone else in the business so that you can see what you're getting into first hand and learn some of the tricks of the trade, what customers need and want, how the business model works and what to charge.

7. Press the flesh
Start networking. This is a great way to develop sales and marketing opportunities by making contact with groups of like-minded business people. It's well recognised nowadays by many business people that networking is a much more cost-effective way of generating new business than traditional marketing activities, such as advertising or public relations. All it really requires is your personal time and energy to do it rather than direct funds from your business. There are many networking possibilities, through local business communities, chambers of commerce, industry events and conferences. And, of course, now we have seen an explosion of online networking opportunities with the emergence of Internet-based business and social networks which allow you to reach people and places that were previously open only to large companies with reach and resources.

8. Prospect

It's never too early to start sales activity. Start putting together lists of sales targets. If you think that you will need it you can buy lists of potential target customers from a variety of database/list providers. For some types of business you might just want to use the old-fashioned approach and go through the Yellow Pages or surf the web for the right sorts of organisations to approach once you are ready to go. However you do it, make sure you do it.

9. Pry

Take a good look at what your direct competitors are doing. Which ones seem to be doing well and which not so well, do they have different market segments that they are trying to reach and do they take a different sales approach? If you are competing with retail outlets then what are their hours of opening, what is their product range, how many staff do they have, do they run pricing promotions? If you're in the construction trade or professional services or cleaning services, find out what marketing activities your competitors are doing to generate customer interest, what their prices are, what their customers think of their service (try asking one or two). If it's feasible, become one of their customers, join their mailing list, subscribe to their website if they have one. By doing some of these things you will gain valuable insight into what is going on in your market and it will help to refine and revise your own Business Proposition and in particular your sales and marketing plans, before you open your doors to your customers.

10. Personal life

Start thinking about how you're going to organise your personal life around the demands that business ownership will bring. Think about what hours you will be expecting to work, where you are going to work and how this will balance with your home life. If you are currently in a job, how about going part-time or taking a sabbatical to give you some time to develop your business without fully committing at this stage? Start to make any arrangements that will be necessary to accommodate these changes, such as childcare provision and house cleaning.

And finally . . .

All of these things should not be undertaken *instead* of spending your precious time and resources on working out your Business Proposition, Business Plan and Financial Forecasts. You will need to make room to do some or all of these things alongside the thinking and writing, planning and preparation activities. You may not want or be able to do all ten suggestions on the Ten P List but we would strongly urge you to try to do at least three or four without fail before you get into the public launch and open your doors for business. And by doing some of them you start to generate some real excitement about your business idea.

Looking ahead, at all times in setting up and running your business, make sure you are continuing to create forward momentum. If you're not moving forwards, then you're almost certainly going backwards because others with whom you are competing will undoubtedly be trying to move forwards and will be getting ahead. Never be complacent about this, always try to be on the front foot.

And this equally applies if you reach the fortunate position where you have set up and established your business and everything seems to be going along just fine. There is a well-known saying that 'if it ain't broke, don't fix it' which most business owners will tend to stick to. But sometimes it's not a bad idea to turn that old maxim on its head and to think in terms of 'if it ain't broke, break it'. Every week you should be asking yourself: 'Is there something else that I could be doing to keep us moving forward, generating momentum, so that we better meet our customers' needs and keep one step ahead of our competition?

LAUNCHING

'The wise man bridges the gap by laying out the path by means of which he can get from where he is to where he wants to go.' J. P. Morgan

So we come to the point of making the big leap and putting your plans into action. In this chapter we describe the launch process – how you can finally bring together all the planning and preparing that you've done into a structured list of things to do to start trading.

Leaving the Shore

If you have followed the stepping-stones to starting up your business this far you will now have done many of the key things that you need to launch your business. You have worked out your proposition, written a Business Plan, decided on your business structure, maybe raised some funding and even tried out a few sales pitches to see what reaction you get. Now it's time to take the final step on the journey to launching your business.

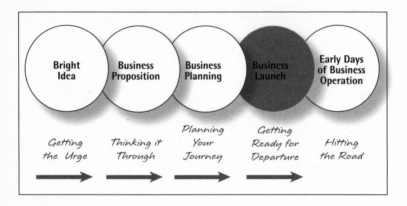

| Bright Idea | Business Proposition | Business Planning | Business Launch | Early Days of Business Operation |

Getting the Urge — Thinking it Through — Planning Your Journey — Getting Ready for Departure — Hitting the Road

Lessons Learned

Over the years, we've been asked to try to help with a number of business launches. In many cases this help was requested because the launch was stalling or failing or in need of some extra help. Usually the management (always enthusiastic, committed, bright people with the right intentions) told us that they've worked out exactly what they want to do and they're all ready to go, they just need to do some marketing and start selling. In many cases it quickly becomes quite clear that the reason they are failing is that they had not carefully thought through their proposition – they had an inadequate view of who their customers were going to be, how they were going to sell and market to them and hadn't investigated properly what their competition was doing. Once we'd managed to persuade them that they weren't quite as far developed as they thought, we would usually then agree with them to go back a few steps and start to think the whole thing through properly.

When Tim and Paul first met a few years ago, Tim was in the advanced stages of launching a business that would provide a range of male grooming products, such as shaving gel, pre-shave cream and aftershave lotion. He had already spent tens of thousands of pounds on developing the liquids and gels, designing packaging, brand creation and website development. The business would sell its products through a mixture of high-end retailers, such as Selfridges, as well as its own website.

But Tim wasn't satisfied that he'd thought it all through properly and so he asked Paul to help him go over everything in detail to make sure all was well. Over a period of a few weeks we worked through much of the process described in this book. We looked thoroughly at the market, the target customers, the products, pricing and proposed sales channels. We put together a simple business model – how the business would make money (or not) and what the key factors in making this venture a success or otherwise would be. We spent time understanding the competition in this market and about how customers made their buying decisions. At the end of about eight weeks Tim made a decision about how to take things forward in light of all this thinking.

Now this is not a story with an entirely happy ending. But it is a story with some good learning points. In Tim's own words: 'After two months of work, we finished thinking about the business on a Friday afternoon and I took myself off to Brighton on my Suzuki 750 on the Saturday morning. I walked around the beach in a bit of a daze for a few hours thinking that what I had put so much time and money into was not going to work and that I would actually throw more good money after bad if I went on. After ordering some mussels on the sea front all the frustration and regret came out and I ended up with tears rolling down into my lunch. I decided then and there to close down the business and to focus on something else.

'My main mistake was that I went from what I thought was a bright idea straight to launching the business but failed to do the necessary steps in between. I had rather naively assumed that if I just created a new product range and put it into the market people would buy it in sufficient quantities to make a successful business. But on proper reflection I came to see that would not be true and probably saved myself at least another £50,000 by doing so.'

By the way, often one of the best things that a mentor can do for a would-be business person is to help them to see why their bright idea may not work in practice and to move on to other ideas, which in this case Tim did.

Launch Process

Some people mistakenly think that a launch simply involves throwing a party where invited guests drink champagne and toast the success of the new venture. This is not the case. By all means have the party, but just remember that when you wake up with a sore head the next day, this is the first day of your new business. Please don't spend too much money on the party because this will just accentuate your headache that will not be alleviated even by aspirin or a hair of the dog that bit you.

Launching your business is a process, not an event. Usually it will require you to complete a list of 'Things To Do' that need to be carried out over a period of time ending with the day that you start doing business with customers. In reality some of them can continue after the launch but here we focus on what's required to get you there. So your launch event, important and great fun though it may be, will be just one of the things to do, and probably a relatively small one at that. You may already have done some of the things that will be required while you have been doing your planning, fundraising and creating momentum, but now it's time to clear the decks and look at what's left to do to start trading.

Launching your business is an exciting time but it is best done in a calm and rational way. Organising what you will need to do requires some sort of structured, orderly and planned sequence to bring you to a point where you are ready to open your door (so to speak) to your first customers. If you plan your launch properly you will save yourself time and money and will avoid making some of the all-too-common mistakes. Take the time to be organised – doing this means that you can be confident that you are really ready and it will save you time and money later.

Launch Plan

You will want your business launch to go smoothly. This will not often happen by accident. There are a thousand things to do before you actually start delivering to customers. So put together a simple project plan to get you from a carefully thought-through Business Proposition to being open for business.

We do not advocate making this overly complicated. But you should put together a launch plan to guide you through all the things that you will need to convert what's in your Business Plan into a fully functioning operation in the real world. Think through all the things that you will need to do to bring your business to life and lay out the steps required in an orderly and sequential fashion. These things might include securing premises, ordering stationary, hiring staff, approaching customers, reaching agreements with suppliers, developing a marketing plan, building your product and arranging a launch event.

There is no single definitive approach to creating a launch plan. The plan can cover a process that can take anything between a few days and many months. We've worked on business launches which took twelve months and involved dozens, sometimes hundreds, of people; others have taken just a few weeks. But they are all basically the same, just on a different scale and even if you are planning to start a very simple business it's worth doing this.

What to Do

Use the launch plan as a tool to manage your way through the launch process. We've provided a simple version of one of these for Styx Jewellery on page 198. Try following these steps:

1   **The Big Picture** – Start with the big picture: what do you want to have in place when you start trading? This could just be a brainstormed list of all the things that you can think of that need to get done

2   **Draft Plan** – Use this list to create a first draft of your plan – you can use the framework we've shown below – get all the main actions that you think that you need to do in some sort of

organised structure. Don't overcomplicate it, just get down the main actions in a rough chronological order to start with. You simply will not be able to see all the things that need to be done before you can launch at this stage but many will emerge over the horizon as you start to move forward. The launch plan is a living document; don't worry if you don't capture everything in the first version of it – you will think of other things and these can be added as you go along. In fact you should be looking at it, going through it in detail just about every day, as it will be your guide to what you need to do today to get everything ready

3   **L–Day** – Decide on an official launch date – call it 'L-Day' or 'D-Day' or whatever you like, but have one in mind. Also decide what you mean by this – is it the day that you start selling or the day that you start delivering orders (you could start selling many days before this), or both? If you're selling a product that will be delivered two months after the customer ordered then you won't need to be ready to deliver on the day that you start selling – you will have a two-month window to build up a sales pipeline. But if you are selling a service like a building trade you may need to be ready to deliver next week. And if you're planning on being in the retail trade you will need everything ready for your customer to visit and buy. Your choice of launch date should be a balance between realistic and stretching – not overly cautious but not stupidly over-optimistic

4   **Milestones** – Identify any other milestone dates that need to be hit along the way if you have any and set those into the launch plan. These might include finalising the lease so that your new premises will be ready in time for your D-Day, arranging for delivery of equipment that takes a few weeks to arrive or having a sign made to put over your shop that cannot be delivered for a month. These milestones will be on what is known as the 'critical path' and are things without which you will not be able to start trading

5   **Review Meeting** – Set a regular time that you and anyone else involved in the business launch with you will meet and review the plan. It's best to do this with someone else rather than try to do it on your own. It's a good tool to use with your mentor but otherwise a friend will do just as well. At the review, go through the plan line by line, ticking off the things that are

complete, finding solutions to actions that have not been completed, adding new actions that have arisen since last time and agreeing what actions need to be done now

6   **Timescales & Responsibilities** – Set timescales, responsibilities and action points for the remaining tasks as well as new tasks that have popped up since your last review. All actions may be yours!

7   **Just Do It** – Go away and get on with your actions; make a note of new things that need to be done and bring those to the next review meeting. Try not to leave all of your actions until the day before the review meeting and then rush around in a blind panic trying to get it all done too quickly

8   **Cycle** – Repeat this process until launch day. With many of the new businesses that we've worked on, we have continued using this project management approach to run the business for weeks and months after the launch because it provides a good management discipline even once you are operational

If you follow this simple process you will find that you are organised and more in control of what can be a hectic and dizzying time even for the most experienced manager.

Marketing Launch

Of the myriad of things that you will need to do leading up to the launch of your business, your marketing activity deserves some special attention. This is how you will make potential customers aware that you have arrived and stimulate their interest and desire to buy from you. You will reap what you sow – if you don't promote what you are doing you will get little response. You should put together a brief marketing plan outlining what you want to achieve with your marketing, how you are going to do it and how much you have got to spend on it.

What do you want to achieve?

The best use of your marketing activity – any budget that you choose to spend on this – will be aimed at generating sales leads. Don't get distracted by thoughts of using marketing to create a brand; at this stage you are just trying to get enough sales to establish your business – building a brand can come much later. Also, there is no point getting your business covered in the media – such as the local paper or on the radio – unless it's actually going to lead directly to sales development. It's very nice getting your photo in the paper but unless it's truly going to generate a sales lead it's probably not worth the effort.

How are you going to do it?

There are many ways to market your business. Here are a few of the possible launch marketing activities that you can do:

- FLYERS – This approach is one of the most popular and effective business marketing tools, particularly for small businesses operating in a limited geographical area. Response rates are often low but this is a relatively low-cost way of putting your business in front of your customers. When you have some spare time you can deliver flyers yourself to keep your costs under control

- ELECTRONIC DIRECT MAIL (EDM) – Email marketing is becoming widespread and can be a cost-effective way to reach your customers. Sending out an announcement that you have arrived can be a great way to make potential customers aware of your business, but beware that there is a high rejection rate of emails sent and many are not willing recipients

- PRESS RELEASES – Writing and sending out a press release to announce your arrival can be a good idea, but if you're going to do this make sure you have an objective in mind. There is little point spending time getting a piece in a national paper if you want to reach customers who do not read a national paper when you are trading in your local community. Make the story interesting if you do go down this road, and always include a photo –

newspaper editors like pictures because it brings the story to life and saves them the cost of sending out a photographer

- ONLINE PROMOTION – These days there is a vast array of promotional opportunity on the web including search engine optimisation, banner advertising and online classified advertising

- SOCIAL NETWORKING PROMOTION – Try to use the range of social and online business networking opportunities that are available to you. Set up your own group and join other groups and consider some of the opportunities available in social networking advertising

Launch event

By all means have one, celebrate your launch but have the following things in the forefront of your mind:

- OBJECTIVES – Make sure you've got some objectives over and above having a good time

- RETURN – Try to work out what return you are going to make from it in hard business terms. Will you find prospective customers from it? Can you get a story in the press from an attending journalist? Do you invite potential investors?

- COMMUNICATE – Ensure those attending know exactly what your business is all about and how they can help you. Don't waste the chance to give them a short presentation of what you do, they will not be expecting a free lunch so take the time to communicate with them. Make sure you tell them clearly what you are doing and what you want from them

We've been to quite a few new business launches – we'll be kind and not mention them by name – where the organisers wasted a golden opportunity to do this. They had invited customers, partners, press and local dignitaries but got a bit too carried away with partying and failed to get the messages across.

Further Thoughts

■ *GET THINGS DONE – Concentrate on getting things done, even if you make some mistakes, do the wrong things and then have to go back later and redo some of them the right way. It's better to be doing things to move you forward and get some wrong than to try to get everything right before moving forward. Success is usually about getting more things right than wrong*

■ *COST MANAGEMENT – During the launch phase you will now be spending money to put your operational capability to sell to and service your customers in place and it's easy to let this expenditure get out of control at this time. Focus rigorously on trying to reduce the costs of anything that you buy from suppliers, even small amounts can add up to the difference between being in the black and running out of cash. Negotiate payment terms where you will pay the supplier as late as possible so that you will preserve your cash until revenue from customers starts to come in and you can better afford to pay*

■ *CASH MANAGEMENT – Similarly, during this period you should keep a very close eye on your finances and in particular the amount of cash that you have – the days before you start making income from your customers are a critical time for your cashflow. This is one of the main times when start-up businesses run out of money. Create a spreadsheet of your cash balance and list of expenditure items made and to be made. Make* sure you are watching what's in the bank and your forthcoming cost commitments carefully

■ TIMES ARROW – When you're in the launch phase of your business time goes by fast – very fast! Make sure you give yourself enough time to get everything done. Don't be too ambitious with your launch date, the world can usually wait a few more days for your great idea, so don't trip yourself up by thinking that you must launch tomorrow. Do it right rather than do it fast and don't put yourself under unnecessary pressure

Styx – Launch Plan Overview

Workstream	Responsible	February				March					April
		01-Feb	08-Feb	15-Feb	22-Feb	01-Mar	08-Mar	15-Mar	22-Mar	29-Mar	05-Apr
Launch Day	n/a										■
Marketing											
Create 'Flyer' Design	John	■									
Write Press Release	Mary		■								
Sales											
Buy customer contact database	John								■		
Start taking orders	John									■	
Suppliers											
Order initial stock	Mary								■		
Set up credit card contract	Mary					■					
Financial											
Sign up with accountant	Mary						■				
VAT registration	Mary					■					
Premises											
Sign lease on offices	John			■							
Buy office furniture	John				■						
Staffing											
Write job description for admin assistant	John					■					
Contact Job Board to place advert	John						■				
Administration											
Set up record keeping book	John							■			
Do filing	John								■		
IT/Equipment											
Buy 2 computers	John		■								
Organise Broadband connection	John		■								

Styx – Launch Plan Overview – Detail of specific work sream – Marketing Work stream

Workstream	Responsible	February				March					April
		01-Feb	08-Feb	15-Feb	22-Feb	01-Mar	08-Mar	15-Mar	22-Mar	29-Mar	05-Apr
Marketing Workstream											
Create 'Flyer' Design	John										
Write Press Release	John								■		
Call Local Newspaper	Mary										
Get Stock photos taken	Mary			■							
Write email to contct list	John										
Send email to contact list	John									■	
Write launch event invitation	Mary							■	■		
Arrange launch event venue	John						■	■			
Write monthly newsletter	Mary										
Send newsletter	Mary				■				■	■	
Complete website	Mary										

HITTING THE
ROAD

EARLY DAYS

'Life's what happens while you are busy making other plans.'
John Lennon

At the beginning of the book we promised to help you to navigate through the first steps that will take you from having a bright idea to being ready to launch. Now that we have reached that destination there are still a few areas where it's really important to focus around the time of your launch. Three key areas that you should concentrate on in the early days of your new business are Selling, Staffing and Supervision.

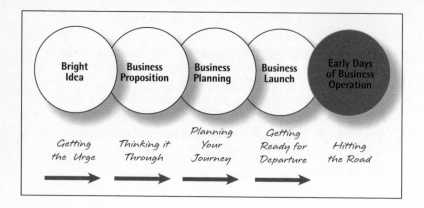

Bright Idea — *Getting the Urge*

Business Proposition — *Thinking it Through*

Business Planning — *Planning Your Journey*

Business Launch — *Getting Ready for Departure*

Early Days of Business Operation — *Hitting the Road*

1. Sales

Whether you're running a multi-national corporation or a hairdressing salon in a local high street, selling your products and services to customers is arguably the most important thing that you can do for your business. Without customers – and the revenue that they generate – you will not have a sustainable business. In our experience of working with many start-up and early stage businesses, it is in this area that most mistakes and the greatest amount of failure take place. In just about every case where an early stage business goes bust it is because an insufficient quantity of sales is being generated, rather than costs being at too high a level. It's always easier to cut costs than to raise revenue, so the latter must be the focus.

Of course other parts of your business are important, like having an informative website, the right equipment and the ability to deliver what you have sold. But these things are all costs. The bottom line is that everything else can take a back seat when it comes to sales because only selling your products and services will generate the income you need to be sustainable. Without sales you have nothing.

Customers will not come to you unless you do something to make this happen – you must be proactive rather than reactive and you must always be on the front foot and go to them. This is so even if you are running a shop where there is a steady footfall of potential customers walking by – think of your shop window display as you being proactive. If you have an e-commerce business don't think that if you create an attractive new website, somehow magically the world will flock to your door. While you are waiting, a competitor will be doing something, leaving you wondering why you haven't got any orders while they are having a nice chat with their new customer. Do not imagine that you are going to be the first person in the history of mankind that is going to defy this golden rule. Many have made that mistake too and no doubt many more will follow. It takes effort, determination, tenacity, persistence and courage to be successful in sales – and you must do it. Unless you are making your sales targets, you are failing.

Like it or not

Unfortunately, many people do not like the idea of selling. For those of you old enough to remember the peak days of the photocopier, double-glazing or life insurance industries, the spectre of a pushy salesperson on your doorstep or in your living room bullying you into signing on the dotted line for something that you didn't really want or need still leaves a bad taste. Some of these people gave selling a bad name. They made customers resistant to hearing about things that really might benefit them because they were terrified that they would be talked into buying things that they didn't want and couldn't afford by the archetypal silver-tongued snake-oil salesman.

As a result, genuine business people have found it more difficult to find a receptive audience and individuals wishing to take up selling as a career are put off by the clichéd image of the salesman in a cheap suit and white socks. And if you can get past this, then there is the fear of having one's efforts rejected and taking this as a personal affront. The thought of selling can also be daunting, particularly if you have limited experience, and this is the main reason why some can be more inclined to get on with things that they are comfortable in doing, rather than push themselves to go out selling.

Fortunately, telling the world about the product or service that you are proud of and passionate about is something that most business owners are quite happy to do. So try to get away from any negative thoughts or the stigma that you may associate with the 'S' word and simply think about it as marketing or promoting the business. Most people are happy enough doing these things and in reality this is much of what selling is about. All you need to do is add a little bit of technique and some management process and you will be doing 'selling'.

Sales can be satisfying and fun. Dealing with your customers, be it at a face-to-face sales appointment, over the telephone or via email is probably the most interesting and rewarding activity that you will do. Customers can be infuriating, funny, impossible, friendly, unpleasant and helpful – all human life is there. But many experienced business owners will tell you that the things they tend to laugh about later revolve around situations that they got involved in with customers. There is no better feeling in business than taking an order for your product or service from a customer and then seeing the payment arrive.

Ten top tips on selling

1   **Ask and you shall receive** – Find out what your potential customers want or need. This is why they say two ears, one mouth: the mouth is equally important as the ears (you will need to talk) but think harder about using your ears – then importantly do something with what you heard. Question and listen. Get into your customers' heads – understand where they are coming from. How do you want to buy things? Think of a seller that you like buying from and think how they go about selling to you

2   **Continuous conversation** – Once you have identified a target customer, find a reason to keep popping up in front of them so that when they are ready you are always in their mind. Be someone that they like to speak with because you give it to them straight, don't beat about the bush. Answer their questions straight. While you may not think that they will want to hear the truth, in the long run this will gain you more than you will lose

3   **Customer lifetime value** – Think of your customers as having a ten-year lifespan with you, not just as a one-off sale. The cost of gaining a new customer is much higher than the cost of keeping an existing one, so go the extra mile to keep a good one. In dealing with your customers' lifetime value, be straight,

think about what you would want. Remember the golden rule: 'Do unto others as you would have others do unto you' – not always infallible because some people don't treat themselves well, but in general empathy usually works

4   **Give them what they want** – Not what you want. Usually you will need to balance what your customer wants – which is often just a bit more than you can do – with what you can genuinely supply. Always be prepared to stretch yourself, but never promise something that you cannot deliver. Make sure that you can deliver what you sold – be sure of this – but don't inhibit a sale by thinking that you'll never deliver it. Stretch yourself even if you have to stay up all night to get the job done

5   **Ever so humble** – You are not in competition with your customer so don't get into any arguments even if you know that you are right – you are there to give them what they want and that you can deliver. By being humble and swallowing your pride you will ultimately win more

6   **Be organised** – The real key to successful selling is being organised and conscientious. Keep good records of your prospects and proposals, personal details about key customer contacts, dates and times to call back and chase. Being systematic and organised is the most important part of an effective sales process

7   **Nice people to do business with** – Be easy to do business with – don't have any policies and procedures that are sales prevention officers. If they want to buy in a certain way, be flexible enough to let them do it that way and tell them that it's a pleasure to do it that way for them. Thomas Edison said: 'Hell, there are no rules here, we're trying to accomplish something'

8   **Practice makes perfect** – Take every opportunity that you can to go out and practise your sales pitch and listen to potential customers. Remember, you should be allocating a considerable proportion of your working week to some aspect of selling, so sometimes, even if it doesn't look like the best prospect, go and do it – you will learn something and get better each time at selling your wares

9   **Deliver what you promise** – Whatever you sell, you must deliver. Experience tends to show that it's usually best to under-promise and then try to over-deliver. Think how you feel as a customer when your expectations have been set by a supplier at a certain level and then they surpass this. Conversely, think how you feel when your expectations are not reached

10   **Don't badmouth** – Never say bad things about your competition. In fact, try to never mention the competition when you're dealing with customers – you don't want to give them any new ideas about going somewhere else. If customers hear you putting your competition down in the dirt they may take the view that while you may be better, you will not need to aim very high to be better

2. Staff

Do you need staff? About 75 per cent of all small businesses in the UK are run by just one person, so only about one quarter will face the issue of when and how to get other people to join them in their business at some stage. Finding and taking on the right staff is one of the biggest challenges facing business owners.

People are the most important asset that your business will possess. Some may argue that this is not always the case, but if you use that as a starting point you will not go far wrong. It's a good mindset to have because it means that you will take this aspect of running your own business as seriously as anything else that you do.

People differ from all other assets in a business because they have thoughts, feelings, motivations and behaviours that are difficult for some to manage. So even the most experienced of business owners and managers can start to get a bit nervous when it comes to hiring new staff. Mistakes can be expensive both financially and emotionally.

As an employer there is a delicate balance to be sought when dealing with staff. On the one hand you will want to treat people like human beings rather than mechanical assets but on the other you need to get the best out of people so you have to get the balance between being nice to them and stretching them and getting them to do what you need done. Typically, your staff haven't got as much invested in your business as you so you can't expect their commitment to match yours – but you can do things to try to encourage this, such as greater involvement in decision making, incentive schemes, share options and so on.

When to staff?

For small businesses, taking on staff is usually more often required in an expansion phase than in start-up but staff may be needed for some businesses from the beginning. However, it's worth outlining what you think you want in the future so that you have this in mind as you start up. Then be prepared to act opportunistically as things develop, always on the lookout should a good person become available to you: if you see someone that you think can do a good job for you (and you think that you can afford them), grab them quickly as good staff are difficult to find. Go the extra mile to offer them what they are looking for. It's always best to be as generous as you can be, without compromising your budgets.

There are a few ways to judge whether or not you need staff. You should be guided primarily by what your Business Plan and Financial Forecast is telling you. But this may change once you get underway and you will inevitably need to adapt due to sales not coming in as quickly as you'd hoped (or quicker) and costs being different to what you'd expected. The two main criteria for deciding on whether to hire staff are:

- *Skills – When you don't have the skills within your business to do what needs to be done*

- *Capacity – When you have the skills but not enough capacity to do the things that need to be done*

There's a judgement to be made about this – you don't want to add staff before you can afford to pay for that person out of revenues coming from your sales, but at the same time if you could take on an additional person now then they might be able to help you generate the sales required to pay for themselves and generate greater revenues and profit. If you have raised funding for your business then some of that can be used to bridge this gap between paying for the new person and the income that they will create. But if you don't have that luxury then you will need to judge the timing carefully. Typically, you will want to generate enough sales to be able to cover the cost of the person before you take them on.

You do also need to be sure that there is a full and demanding job for the person to do as there is nothing worse than starting a new job only to find that there is not really a full-time job to do. And when you do take them on make sure they are fully occupied – better for them to say they are overloaded and for you to deal with that than see them using Facebook for hours each day.

At all stages, run until you are starting to feel like you are creaking at the seams, where the quality of your customer service may start to suffer. But don't go beyond breaking point because it could be hard to recover from that. Also remember that it takes six to eight weeks to recruit someone so build that in to your timing. Overall, it's most important not to take people on too soon. This is a very common mistake and often leads to finding that they were not required anyway.

If you think that you do need additional human resource, start off by considering whether a subcontractor on a pay-as-you-go basis could provide what you need. This will help you keep your costs under control (although you may pay more per hour than for the equivalent full-time member of staff) and limit your risk – you can always ask them to stop at any time without being in the position of having to pay notice, holidays or redundancy. You will also save on employers' National Insurance contributions as these are not paid to this type of manpower.

If you want to work out the economics of this a simple way is to say that a full-time employee works for approximately 228 days per year

(365 days less 25 days holiday entitlement less 8 days public holidays less 104 days at weekends = 228 days). Now divide their annual pay by 228. Say it's £25,000 ÷ 228 = £110 per day. You need to add on a bit for National Insurance but that's close enough to make the comparison with the cost of a contractor.

You will often hear it said that good people are hard to find and yet we all know any number of 'good' people, so why does this seem to cause such a problem? Business owners tend to have high standards of how they want things to be done. Many find that others cannot quite do things as well as they do them for themselves, or at least in the same or a similar way. So they worry that their customers will not get quite as good a service as they would want. Often they can feel out of control, not quite sure what's going on now that they are not doing a particular task any more. And then when they do hire someone, they have to invest so much of their own time in getting them up to speed, showing them what needs to be done and how they want things doing that they think that they might as well just do it themselves. You might find that you will become less productive than before you hired the new person, at least until you have got them up to speed. These are all perfectly understandable anxieties but, in the end, if you are planning on growing you will need to find ways to get new people into your business and trust them to get on with things.

Top tips on staffing

1   **Specify well** – Clearly specify what role you want fulfilling and the type of person you are looking for to carry out that role

2   **Network** – Use your network of contacts to find people before you advertise vacancies, but be careful about taking on your family and friends

3   **Known quantities** – Try to recruit people that you've worked with before and know what they can and can't do and . . .

4   **Referrals** – Recruit people who are referred to you by people whose opinions you respect – bear in mind that this can cause embarrassment if things go wrong, but it is a good way to take the risk out of your recruitment

5   **Small business experience** – Take on people that are comfortable and experienced in working in small business. There is a chasm between working for a big company with all its resources and what's required day to day in a small business and this can cause problems for those who are not used to it

6   **Interview well** – Prepare your questions well and think hard about what you want to know and why you are asking. Try to ask questions which find out how candidates acted in a certain situation and why, in order to determine how they may act in a similar situation in future

7   **Reward** – Provide the best compensation package that you can afford – this means being as generous as you can within your limited budget to get the right person. There is no point trying to save a few pennies if you lose someone you want

8   **Welcome** – Run an induction programme – this doesn't have to be anything fancy but a good introduction to your business, the market, other staff, how you do things, your processes and policies and what you are expecting from them. People really appreciate this

9   **Don't rush** – Don't take on just anybody because you have an urgent problem to deal with. Take as much time as it takes to get the right person – it costs you to get them and sometimes even more to get rid of them, so delay rather than rush it. Act in haste, repent at leisure

3. Supervision

Setting the direction

After all the planning and preparation, all the thinking, the setting up and getting ready to launch, you have finally set out on the day-to-day operation of your business. How do you know that you're going in the right direction and how can you keep control of things? As far as direction goes, sticking rigidly to your Business Plan is one answer but you will find out that things can change quickly – and you will need to evolve or become extinct. You will almost certainly find yourself being forced by events to start deviating from your original plans, sometimes just to stay afloat and also to make the most of opportunities as they arise. So how do you go about deciding upon and then staying with your chosen direction?

Keeping control requires attention to detail and a methodical approach. You need to get the balance right here. Some business owners are quite content to spend a large amount of time setting up an accounting system and then closely monitoring every penny going in and out of their business, while sometimes neglecting other activities, such as sales and marketing, that are essential for success. Beware of becoming the lonely miser sitting in your tower counting your money. Conversely, many (probably most) business owners find this 'boring admin' the least desirable part of business life. They tend to leave it until it's either too late, by which time they may have run out of money without realising it, or do it just in the nick of time but then have to invest several days in getting things under control or having to pay someone else to do it for them.

In reality a little bit of common sense and a small amount of discipline can go a long way when it comes to keeping on track and under control. Here are some approaches that can help you achieve this:

Annual Plan

Take a look at your Business Plan. You will know much of this off by heart by now and many of the things that it says will have been implemented to get you to this point. As we said earlier, business plans are out of date almost as soon as you have finished them, which by this stage may have been some weeks or months ago. Of course, it will still guide your strategy and be your business roadmap, but you now have to get into the detail of running the business.

So now it's time to put together an action plan that will set out in simple terms what you are going to aim to achieve in the first period of operation after launch – decide a period of 30, 60 or 90 days. Your new plan, we'll call it your Annual Plan, will be based on all your original thinking and will be closely aligned with that. What it contains will vary depending upon your specific type of business. There are many ways that you can do this but we would suggest that you think about including the following three components:

1   **Your Business Priorities** – What are the key things that you want to achieve over the next period of time?

2   **Key Activities and Responsibilities** – What things need to be done to achieve your business priorities and who is responsible for doing them?

3   **Timing and Budget** – When do these things need to be done and how much will you spend on them?

The table right shows the kind of things that a new small business might plan to do over its first 30, 60 or 90 days after launch.

Why do an Annual Plan?

- *GUIDE YOU – To ensure that you have a direction and that you are able to share the objectives with others who are going to be helping you achieve them*

- *MANAGE YOUR PRIORITIES – Focus on a few critical issues; if you are tempted to get distracted away from this core plan, that's fine if you like, but make sure you do all the things in the plan*

- *ASSIGN RESPONSIBILITIES – Make someone accountable for the achievement of each task*

- *TRACK PROGRESS REGULARLY – Tell yourself when you need to do something to get back on track*

- *MANAGE YOUR CASH – Ensure that everything you do is within the available cash at your disposal*

Keeping control

Keeping control of your business is critical for sustained success. To keep control you will need visibility of what is going on. This means not burying your head in the sand, having some sort of system to show you how things are going (not a complicated one), and keeping good records and up to date with the paperwork. As we said above, this is not always the favourite preserve of the business owner – we

Annual Plan Summary – example

Business Priorities	Key Activities and Responsibilities	Costs	Timing
Acquire 10 new customers per month	Run a sales campaign	n/a	April–June
	Set up freephone telephone line to handle enquiries	£500 p.a.	April
	Hire sales person to drive campaign	£25,000 p.a.	March
	Create website	£2,500 one-off	March
	Create sales brochures	£100 p.a.	April
Generate 100 sales leads in 3 months	Identify target customers	n/a	June
	Buy lists or targets	£500	June
	Prepare flyers	n/a	July
	Deliver flyers to targets	£500	August
Hire 2 staff to handle sales and servide delivery	Write job descriptions	n/a	June
	Place advertisements	£2,000	June
	Interview and hire	£18,000 annual salary for each new staff member	July–August
	Develop and run induction course	n/a	September
Move into new premises	Appoint agent to find options. Produce summary of your requirements and budget	£15,000 per year	October
Raise £5,000 in funding to develop a new product line	Update business plan. Research sources of funding. Set up meetings. Prepare 'pitch' presentation	Zero budget allocated	November

usually hear the tired old 'I haven't got time for that' excuse. But this is no excuse. Make time and you will reap the benefit of this investment. You wouldn't drive your car without looking at your dashboard to check your speed, temperature or fuel indicator – so don't think about running your business without setting yourself up with some basic indicators – a dashboard – to show you what's going on.

Top ten areas to keep control

1   **Cash** – Once you have your budget you will then need to try to stick to it, because once your cash has gone it may be even harder to raise more. Some businesses run out of cash before they even get to the end of their road when they might well have had what was needed to be successful but just ran out of money before it could be realised

2   **Sales** – Sales are your life-blood without which you have no income, so set up a regular sales review meeting, even if this is just you alone, and go through all your targets, prospects and any proposals that you have issued. Make an action list of things to do to follow through on these

3   **Costs** – Don't spend your cash on anything non-essential, especially before you have customers. Money is a precious commodity and it always disappears faster than you expected. Get someone else, such as your mentor, to regularly challenge you and hold you to account on what you are spending your cash on

4   **Bank Account** – Monitor your cash balance carefully and regularly, look at it every day if possible, at least until you have a large enough bank balance that you no longer need to watch it so closely

5   **Expenses** – Keep all your receipts for expenditure incurred for things for your business. You will need to provide them as evidence that you spent this money and they may be required for an inspection by HMRC to justify your claim that they were for the business

6   **Time** – Take time to manage your time. Force yourself to commit some proportion of your time each week to deal with sales, marketing, staff, finances and administration and allow some time, even if it's just a short period, for thinking about things – how you are doing, where new opportunities lie, how you could improve things

7   **Records** – Make sure that you keep good records of all the business's transactions. You will need either a spreadsheet or handwritten page of all your invoices and payments, bank transactions, petty cash payments, purchases from suppliers and VAT collected and reclaimed. If you have staff you will need to keep records of payroll payments, tax deductions and National Insurance payments

8   **Suppliers** – While you may be happy with your current suppliers, make sure that you are continuously looking at what else is available and looking for ways to improve what you receive and to reduce costs

9   **The Government** – There are a number of legal requirements, such as making an annual return and filing a set of annual accounts if you are a company or getting a tax return in if you are a sole trader. Do not neglect these things, stay on top of them. Government departments can take a dim view of your lack of communication with them. An accountant can relieve you of much of this burden

10 **Time Out** – Make sure that you give yourself regular breaks away from the business, even if these are only short ones. This is not just to recharge your batteries but is essential to give you the space to get your head above the trees for the generation of new ideas, problem solving and creative thinking

WRONG TURNS

'Anyone who has never made a mistake has never tried anything new.' Albert Einstein

In this chapter we take a look at some of the common mistakes made in the early stages of starting a business and provide some signposts to help you keep on the right path.

Same Old Mistakes

Rather like the politicians who claimed to have abolished economic boom and bust, there is always a new generation of business owners who come through believing that they will be the first to get it all right and make no mistakes this time. One day, when the Earth has cooled, they may be right, but for the time being it's probably just as well to take the view that most of the mistakes that have been made in the past are still relevant today, and that you would be wise to heed these and learn from them.

There are many things that can go wrong in the start-up phase and early stages of your new business. Some of these you might be able to do something about while others will be outside your control. Often these can seem like complete dead ends or roadblocks that will force you to turn back or give up. They can appear impossible to overcome. Don't be discouraged, there is usually a solution to every problem and one of the keys to success is to continue to try to find a way of overcoming blockages, staying determined not to give up.

Making some mistakes and learning from them is an important part of the business ownership journey and gaining some of these scars is an essential part too. But there are some frequently committed start-up atrocities that are so common and so obviously avoidable that they are worth describing so that you can at least consider doing something about them before they do something unpleasant to you. So, here are some basic 'schoolboy errors' and how to avoid them:

1   Cash Conservation

2   Demand Delusion

3   Focus on a Few

4   Conspicuous Consumption

5   Strive for Sales

6   Channel Conflict

7   Making Changes

8   Time Management

9   Share Your Ideas

1. Cash conservation

Failure to carefully manage your cash is a major reason for business failure.

We have seen earlier the importance of cash to your business. It is the oil that runs the engine – while you have it you can pay the bills and buy the things you need to operate the business. Run out of it and the engine will seize up, potentially bringing things to a grinding halt and ending in insolvency. Just about every start-up or early stage business has limited cash with which to work. You never have quite enough money to do what you want to do. This is usually viewed as a bad thing: 'If only I had more money and the people or equipment it could buy us then we could be more successful.' But in many ways it's a good discipline to have. While a fortunate few may have raised funds to help them get started, this can also run out if not carefully managed. We have seen too many potentially good businesses go under because they ran out of money to keep them going before they executed their plan fully and started to generate the revenues from customers.

Conserving your cash is key. From the beginning be very careful with every penny that you spend. Only spend money on things that are essential to the success of the business. This requires judgement on your part because it's often easy to find a reason to spend. You do not need clever software programs to do this, just keep a Cashflow Forecast up to date and look at your bank account regularly to see what's coming in and what's going out. Be careful to manage when payments leave – while not upsetting your suppliers by making late payments – and try to synchronise these with the receipt of payments from your customers. If you do need to make a delayed payment let your supplier know, don't just ignore it and bury your head in the sand. Most people are reasonable about giving you a few more days as long as you let them know what's going on.

You need to match your business expenditure to your business performance. Set yourself a tight budget, in line with your Business Plan. Spend the minimum amount required to get you going, no more. Bootstrap your way through the early days matching your outgoings with income from your customers. Once you have your first customers, then you can start to think about acquiring a few more of the things that you might want. Get your mentor to review this with you; be hard on yourself. Try to get things for nothing. Beg and borrow (don't steal), make do with less than what you would like until you can afford better.

2. Demand delusion

Incorrectly believing that your product or service will be in great demand or that you will sell enough to be sustainable is a big mistake.

Are you really sure that customers will want what you are proposing to offer, and in sufficient quantities to make your business sustainable? Many have misjudged this in the past and paid the price. It's easy to start believing that what your business offers will be immediately demanded by hordes of eager customers. Do not believe that if you build it, they will inevitably come or that you are the only game in town. Customers were probably quite happily getting on with their lives before you came along and unless you have something that will motivate them to buy from you they will not even know that you exist. And they will go on happily enough without you – the graveyards are full of people who thought they were indispensable. One of the biggest errors people make is to over-exaggerate the need for what you have to offer. So don't fool yourself; retain some humility.

Many times we've seen early stage businesses that have developed a new product or service and been told by its creator that this is the next big thing. They may have built it, but does anyone want to buy it? Avoid solutions trying to solve a problem. In the 1980s Sinclair Research, a highly entrepreneurial company, notoriously introduced an electric bike (called the Zike), a piece of technology that looked like a cross between a go kart and a bobsleigh in which you sat back and pedalled around the busy streets. No doubt it was technologically very clever and invented by a man who had pioneered home computing in the UK. But it was a commercial failure – it sold about 2,000 units. Whilst it may succeed now, at that time there was an insufficient market demand to allow it to succeed.

3. Focus on a few

Trying to offer too wide a range of products and services, particularly at an early stage, will force you to spread your limited resources too thinly and can lead to failure.

Focus heavily on what you do best. If you're selling products, start with a limited number. If you provide a service, start off doing what you know that you can deliver well and consistently; don't try to do things that you are less certain about. Start with just one or two things and try to be really good at those. Don't try to expand what you are doing too quickly. There is potentially an endless number of opportunities that you can explore but you must judge carefully which ones you are going to put time and resources into. Only do this in a very slow and steady way or you will lose focus on your core business – the one that you started in the first place – and run the risk of it falling over while you chase after exciting new but unproven ideas. If you do expand, do it in such a way that you are keeping close to your existing or core offers so that you can build on solid foundations in an area that you know about and can manage.

4. Conspicuous consumption

Spending money is easy and too many fall into the trap of finding good excuses as to why they just need to spend on one thing or another in order to make their business work.

Freshly armed with a new bank account and some start-up funding, the enthusiastic business owner rushes out to procure all those essential items without which their business will not be able to function, buying the company car or taking an office complete with nice furnishings or acquiring the latest gadgets and gizmos which will be ever so useful at some stage. Typical candidates for this expenditure are a flash new website, colourful business cards, printed stationery, company mugs, membership of a club (so that we can hold customer meetings there of course). And with the added bonus that all this expenditure can be offset against tax and that the VAT on it can be claimed back.

Among all the other good reasons not to do this kind of thing (see Cash Conservation above) is the fact that your customers will see this going on and will rightly ask themselves the question: 'Who is paying for all this consumption?' In many cases the answer is that it's they as the customer who is paying. Some of them will assume that you are obviously charging too much if you can afford to splash the cash in all directions. And then they might take the view that perhaps they can get the same thing cheaper from somewhere else. So, be careful about appearing flashy. It's not big and it's not clever. The best businesses are low key and careful when it comes to conspicuous consumption.

5. Strive for sales

Lack of sales is the single biggest killer of new businesses. Invest inadequate time and effort in achieving sales and you will quickly join the thousands that have failed in the past.

We've already said much about the dangers of being cautious when it comes to sales activity. Lack of income from sales to customers is the single biggest thing that sends businesses to the wall. When you start running your own business there are a multitude of things to do with your time. Many of them may be very interesting and seemingly important. Some of them you really like doing – after all, that may be why you started in this line of business in the first place. Whatever else you distract yourself with, don't avoid sales activity and don't be cautious or hide your light under the proverbial bushel. Get out your wares in full public view and sell. Allocate a large proportion of your time to sales-related activities, even if you have hired others to handle sales – they will need managing. That means in any given working week you should be able to say that you are putting at least a couple of days purely into sales effort. Engage in sales lead generation every week – make calls, distribute flyers, use online networks, advertise, speak at conferences, try to get some free publicity in your local paper.

6. Channel conflict

Many early stage businesses that give up control of their sales effort realise this mistake too late and pay the price.

Sales strategy for early stage businesses should be based mainly on selling your product or service yourself and not throwing it over the wall to a third party to do so on your behalf. Don't rely solely on third parties to sell your products and services until you are established, have proven that your product or service sells and can afford the resource to manage the third party. As an early stage business it's usually best to try to sell directly to your customers as the default position, although of course some business models require selling through third parties, such as retailers or distributors. Even in that case it can be helpful to try to sell at least some of what you offer directly yourself – try setting up a website or taking a market stall. This is because you will have control over how your product or service is being offered and you will be able to get immediate reaction to what you are offering and so be able to modify and improve it if required. When you sell through others you lose much of this valuable insight and can feel isolated from what is happening and out of control. While it is important to get your sales channels sorted out from the beginning, be prepared to adjust quickly if they're not working as you want them to.

We worked with a company that had great new technology in the rapidly growing 'cloud computing' market. This is currently one of the major shifts in technology that is driving new businesses, products and services in the IT world. There are enormous opportunities to create new businesses here as millions of customers change from having all their computing applications on the hard drive of their computer to a model where applications are accessed from a remote server (the cloud) via high-speed Internet connections. One of the great challenges of this approach to computing is security. The customer is in one place (potentially many places if they use a laptop) and their data and applications are a long way away on a remote server – how can you ensure that no one else can intercept things that are going backwards and forwards between the two? The answer to this need lies in strong 'authentication' and 'encryption' services. This is what this company provided. So, a new business in this field should be a winner, shouldn't it? While the business was in a rapidly expanding market and had a great solution to a big problem, it failed after about three years of trying. Why? Their idea and product was good but they wrongly decided to sell it through third-party distributors and retailers from the outset rather than doing it directly themselves. After a few months of low sales they eventually investigated what was happening in their distributors and discovered that they were just one of thousands of products being sold – no one was trying to sell their product. Sadly, this company ran out of money before it could get established and eventually went out of business.

7. Making changes

Being inflexible and stuck in the mud about what your business does and how it does it is not recommended.

You will need to be constantly thinking about reinventing your business so as to keep up with the inevitable trends and changes in the markets and with your customers' needs and wishes and moving with market trends. Spend some time every month thinking about how you could improve and develop what you offer: should you introduce new products, is your pricing competitive or does it need a tweak, can you do a sales promotion for a period of time, is your website up to date or is it looking a bit tired? Obviously this needs to be balanced with doing business as usual and you should not be looking to totally change things around every few weeks or months, but carefully thought-through and implemented improvements are an essential part of continuing success.

8. Time management

Planning your time so that you proactively give enough attention to key activities is essential.

Given that the large majority of small businesses consist of only one or two people, it's critical that you manage your time effectively. This will not just happen by chance or accident. You will need to actively do something to make it happen. Lack of time management is a typical inhibitor of success in start-up and early stage businesses, affecting companies with management teams as well as one-person firms. The owner-manager never seems to have any time to do anything yet cannot seem to put their finger on what they are spending all their time doing.

This is a key area for you to work on with your mentor – it often takes someone looking from the outside to see what you are doing and get you to realise this and adapt your behaviour. Ask yourself: 'What am I doing with my time each week?' Work out a time-management plan – preferably with your mentor if you have one – it doesn't need to be anything complicated. Try to allocate chunks of time each week to important activities, such as sales or recruitment or managing your finances. If you put these stakes in the ground it will free up time for you to deal with the urgent and unplanned things that inevitably arise when you are sometimes least expecting them.

9. Share your ideas

Don't be over-protective of your business idea – there is not much new in the world and your success will be based on your ability to deliver, not the idea itself.

Whether you're in the planning stage, looking for funding or fully operational, don't keep you business idea to yourself. As we said earlier, there are very few truly original new ideas so don't think that by keeping yours to yourself you are protecting it from being stolen. Nobody will be interested in doing this. It's much better to give your proposition the oxygen of a public airing – it will start to breathe if you share it with others and get their feedback on it, good, bad or (worst of all) indifferent. If you're looking for funding most external investors are not particularly interested in signing confidentiality agreements (venture capital companies will hardly ever do this). By sharing what you are up to you are more likely to get people interested and willing to help you.

15 THE JOURNEY CONTINUES

'In my beginning is my end, in my end is my beginning.'
Thomas Stearns Eliot

The End of the Beginning

All of which brings us nearly to the end of this journey through the main steps required to take you from your initial desire to run your own business through to a well-planned and worked-out proposition. You're ready to launch.

But this is merely the start for you if you have read this far – the end of one part of the journey and the beginning of the next. You now need to get on with the day-to-day adventures of making your business great.

The approaches that we've covered in this book are tried and tested over many years. Using them will not guarantee that you will be successful with your business but they will improve your chances of success and importantly will stop you from making many of the mistakes along the way that we, and many others, have made.

We cannot stress enough the value of carefully considering whether or not this is the right life for you before you make the jump. We have tried to give you a feel for what you can expect to do and gain from the experience of setting up your own business as well as pointing out the drawbacks and downsides that will be encountered. Business ownership is not for everyone and it's not true to say that anyone can do it – it simply isn't everyone's cup of tea and can cause more harm than good when undertaken by those for whom it's not right or who are ill prepared.

At the heart of this book is the principle that you should spend time working out the three main pillars of any new business – your Business Proposition, Business Model and a Business Plan. You should always do these things as they are the solid rocks upon which you will build and develop your business.

But businesses should not and cannot be created in an ivory tower, beautifully planned in minute detail but completely detached from the real world. So we have talked a lot about the multitude of things that you can and should just get on with to create momentum for your business. The challenge that we all face in creating new businesses is to get the balance right between running off and getting on with it and thinking it all through properly before committing time and money.

There is not a black and white solution to doing this – it's about using the right approaches, tools and techniques and then applying your judgement of what to do and when to do it. Just remember that you need to both plan carefully and get on with things – don't neglect either of them.

While it's all well and good to read about this in a book, in practice doing these things is made much easier if you have others to do them with. We have pointed out the huge benefit that you will get from working with a business mentor even if you are part of a team that is developing a business together. You will find that a good business mentor will understand much of the guidance written in these pages and can help to further expand upon it and make it specific to your business. So we strongly recommend that you find someone to assist you in this way.

Success in business is never guaranteed and the quest to ensure that any business survives and prospers is a daily one for all owners, shareholders, directors, managers and employees. But while the pursuit of profit is paramount, there is more to it than just success and failure in these terms. Over the decades millions of people have changed their lives through the process of starting up and running their own businesses. Every year thousands more take this path. They have found that it has given them independence, the chance to make a difference, control over their working life and the chance to make a good living while they're doing it.

Nowadays starting up and running a business is open to just about everyone, regardless of where they come from, their family background, age, education, race or gender. Business rewards individuals who take responsibility for themselves and their actions, being committed and determined to succeed even when it gets tough – which it almost certainly will – and caring about others, such as customers and employees. It rewards those who want to prove something to themselves and occasionally those who want to prove others wrong.

And business can be great fun. Having your own business can change your life and help you to develop as a person. Of course it requires a great deal of hard work, a willingness to learn and an ability to put up with the highs and lows, but it can give you much more than you get in return than many of the jobs working for others. There are times when it can be uncomfortable, but there are many times also when the satisfaction and rewards can be great, with a lot of fun to be had along the way. And it's in that spirit that this book is written.

INDEX

Note: Page numbers in **bold** denote major sections.